DATE DUE

			PRINTED IN U.S.A.

D1559682

THE SECRET SOLUTION

How One Principal
Discovered the Path to Success

Todd Whitaker, Sam Miller, and Ryan Donlan

Illustrations by Eric Cleveland and Ryan Donlan

Rowman & Littlefield Education
A division of
ROWMAN & LITTLEFIELD PUBLISHERS, INC.
Lanham • New York • Toronto • Plymouth, UK

Published by Rowman & Littlefield Education
A division of Rowman & Littlefield Publishers, Inc.
A wholly owned subsidiary of The Rowman & Littlefield Publishing Group, Inc.
4501 Forbes Boulevard, Suite 200, Lanham, Maryland 20706
www.rowman.com

10 Thornbury Road, Plymouth PL6 7PP, United Kingdom

British Library Cataloguing in Publication Information Available

Library of Congress Cataloging-in-Publication Data
Whitaker, Todd, 1959-
  The secret solution : how one principal discovered the path to success /
Todd Whitaker, Sam Miller and Ryan Donlan.
    p. cm.
  ISBN 978-1-4758-0613-7 (cloth : alk. paper) -- ISBN 978-1-4758-
0614-4 (pbk. : alk. paper) -- ISBN 978-1-4758-0615-1 (electronic) 1.
School principals. 2. Educational leadership. 3. School management and
organization. 4. Educational change. I. Title.
  LB2831.9.W44 2013
  371.2'012--dc23

                                        2013033318

⊗™ The paper used in this publication meets the minimum requirements of
American National Standard for Information Sciences—Permanence of Paper
for Printed Library Materials, ANSI/NISO Z39.48-1992.

Printed in the United States of America

CAST OF CHARACTERS OF ANYWHERE MIDDLE SCHOOL

(IN ORDER OF THEIR APPEARANCE, IN A TOWN NEAR YOU)

Roger Rookie—New principal of Anywhere Middle School.

Carol Charming—Eager young local newspaper reporter.

Ned Neverthere—Former principal who was a bit out of touch.

Nellie Newcomer—New enthusiastic teacher, ready to make a difference.

Mildred Morose—Negative veteran staff member who thrives on "a following."

Judy Slacker—Veteran teacher whose last name says it all.

Karl Chameleon—Eighth-year math teacher who goes with the flow.

LaVon Babble—If it isn't good enough, it wouldn't be the minimum.

Trudy Savage—Office secretary and executioner. Just try to take a box of paper clips without asking. Just try!!

Kris Bliss—The personable, friendly front office receptionist.

Sandy Starr—The most respected and effective teacher in the school.

Edgar Sleeper—Social studies teacher, losing his luster as he hangs with a toxic crowd.

Joel Gerrymander—Roger's friend, principal/athletic director from neighboring school, schmoozer, manipulator, and high-speed multi-tasker. Shoots "Fire, Ready, Aim!"

Cindy Sage—Superintendent's secretary of thirty years: dignified, maternal, and wise.

Ivan Ironside—Ex-military captain and neighboring town's current middle school principal. Don't mess around with this guy.

TABLE OF CONTENTS

❶

THE BIG NIGHT

Tonight was Roger Rookie's big night.

He couldn't believe it! He was about to be recognized as this year's "Super Apple" award winner by the state principals' association, and even given a shiny trophy! Boy, was he proud. He kept reminding himself to make sure he thanked his teachers in his acceptance speech. They had worked so hard and had come so far. He knew that winning this award was a team sport.

As Roger sat quietly in a small room adjacent to the ceremony, the door opened and in walked Carol Charming from the big newspaper in town.

Wow! The local reporter is here to ask ME some questions! Roger beamed.

Carol walked over to Roger and shook his hand. "I'm pleased to meet you, Mr. Rookie."

"As am I, Ms. Charming, and please call me 'Roger.'"

"Only if I'm 'Carol.'"

"You got it, Carol."

"Well, Roger, you have a big night ahead of you. Would you have a few minutes to talk?"

"Certainly, I don't think I'm on for about another fifteen or twenty minutes."

He thought to himself, *She seems very nice. I hope I make a favorable impression.*

Carol was surprised at how young Roger looked.

"I'd like to start, Roger, by saying 'Congratulations.' You must be so proud of receiving one of the highest honors in the entire state. I bet as well that everyone at Anywhere Middle School feels lucky to have you as principal. This must come so easy for you. What is your secret?!?"

Roger half smiled, looked at Carol, paused, and said, "I asked myself that same question probably one hundred times, Carol. And if you would have seen me in my first year, you would never have used the word 'easy'! I wasn't sure I was going to make it through my first week!"

"No way," said Carol.

"Yes, way!" Roger chuckled.

"I've got to be honest. At first, I wasn't even sure who I really was as a leader. I just thought of survival. Trust me, no one would have ever guessed I would ever be on stage getting an award for doing something positive. I didn't have a clue. I tried on different styles of leadership, all while searching for the path to success. Searching for the 'secret.'"

Carol seemed startled by his response.

She said, "I would have never guessed you struggled starting out. How did you go from that sort of start to being today's award winner? Especially in just two years! I'd love to hear more!"

Roger laughed, "To say I struggled would be a huge understatement. I figured that the only award I might get was the 'Shortest Stint as a Principal.' Let me tell you a story about how I started and where I've come."

"That would be great!" said Carol. "Education's my favorite beat. I LOVE to report great news on schools, especially the *'Come from Behind'* kind!!"

Roger Rookie's thoughts moved backward, taking him and Carol Charming on a journey from the award ceremony to his telephone ringing just two years prior.

A CALL FROM THE BOSS

Ring . . . ringgg . . . ringgggggg.
"Hello, Roger Rookie here."

It was Roger's superintendent.

"Rookie, as soon as you're done unpacking, I want to see you in my office."

"Yes sir, I'll be right over."

Roger dropped everything and hurried right to the Office of the Superintendent.

"Rookie," the superintendent began, "You're an impressive kid with what I believe to be a lot of potential, but I don't have a lot of time for your care and feeding. I have board members all over me who want results."

"Results, sir?"

"Yeah, results! Learning results!"

"What I need you to do immediately in Anywhere Middle School is to turn around that school, plain and simple. I want the school to value the learning that goes on, not just the teaching. And at this point, Rookie, I don't even think AMS values its teaching as much as it does its *teachers*! We're not here to create salaries for adults, young man; we're here for the learning of children! I want results, not just 'forming a committee <u>this</u>' or 'meeting with stakeholders <u>that</u>' . . . I want that place turned around."

"And Rookie . . . I want accountability. No time to cry about the labor pains . . . just show me the baby! Test results are in the tank. Every SINGLE time that Lois Lane upstart from our local newspaper writes another story, it seems that the school down the road looks better than ours. I think her name's Charming . . . CAROL CHARMING."

"Should I develop a relationship with her, sir?"

"I don't care what you do in your spare time, Rookie, just keep it out of the headlines."

"I meant . . ."

"Rookie, they say Charming has a nose for news. Well, I'll tell you she has a nose all right, because she's always sniffin' around for something. Usually, it's evidence of student learning. Test scores, particularly. Darn it, when we serve up our standardized test scores the next time around, I want them smelling like roses!!"

"They will, sir!" Roger snapped.

"That's what I want to hear, kid, 'cause I'm tired of looking like a fool. Not gonna happen any longer!"

"No it won't, sir."

"You got smart people working there. I know . . . I hired most of them. Some I even taught with, back in the day. Something's wrong, though . . . not sure what it is, but that place just doesn't seem to value learning like it did when I taught there."

"I'll figure it out, sir."

"Darn tootin' you will, Rookie! Find out what it is, and fix it. Don't spend a lot of money either! When Neverthere was principal, every time I asked him a question, it seemed that he didn't even know what was going on in those classrooms. Can't figure out why! Seemed to have a good head on his shoulders, that Neverthere. But he was clueless!!!"

"I'll try to have a clue, sir."

"You bet you will, Rookie! Son, you got your marching orders. Any questions?!?"

"No, sir. I'll get that school whipped into shape in no time. I'll figure out the secret! I'll find that path toward a focus on learning. You can count on Roger Rookie."

SHINY NEW OFFICE

The sign on the door at Anywhere Middle School (AMS) read, *Mr. Roger Rookie, Principal.* Being a brand new principal, Roger smiled every time he saw his name on the door. Sometimes he even said it to himself, "Principal Rookie." It had a nice ring to it.

When no one was looking, Roger would take the cuff of his shirt and kind of polish the nameplate so it looked nice and shiny. Looking at his reflection, Roger would then point and say, "You da man!"

This was his first job as a school administrator; he was stoked.

Roger always knew he wanted to be an educator. He started college with a clear focus as a future teacher, a future difference maker. College only deepened his excitement. He loved his classes (at least most of them). He learned a lot (at least from most professors) and was so excited when he finally had the chance to practice teaching in his senior year.

I was the best darn thing to happen to education in quite some time, he mused. *You da man!*

Plus . . . he was geeked the first time someone called him "Mr. Rookie."

I can even put that on my business cards, he toyed. *Well, if teachers had business cards.*

The teacher who supervised Roger during his student teaching internship, Mr. Indifferent, was closing in on retirement. He saw Roger as "free labor" and allowed Roger to take over the classroom entirely on just his second day!

There were some missteps, of course, but "Mr. Rookie" gradually won over the students and developed a balance between building relationships and high expectations. He was a go-getter and started applying for teaching jobs early in his final semester.

Through good fortune and hard work, I'll have my first teaching position before graduation day! Roger promised himself.

And he did!!!

Roger Rookie loved teaching and soon learned that he could make an even bigger impact on his students by continuing his education. He started a master's degree program in school administration because it looked like fun. Plus, all the older guys (none administrators . . . they were just in it for the pay increase) told stories about weekend classes, some even held at hotels in destination cities. Food . . . drinks . . . not too much homework. Yep . . . lots of fun!!!

I'll say this, the classes are sure interesting, Roger thought at the time. *A principalship might be something I'll do if I get tired of teaching. It seems as though the principals I have known have all been a little tired of something.*

It turns out the timing was right! Just when Roger was graduating from principal school, the district adjacent to where he taught announced that its principal was to retire. Friends joked with him that he should put all that tuition money to good use and throw his hat into the race. Roger knew that he wouldn't even get past the first round because that particular district always hired from within. Even the superintendent used to teach there.

Most thought it cute that he applied, even his mom.

He was SOOO young!

Peer pressure and a bit of friendly banter from his friend, Joel Gerrymander, an athletic director/assistant principal in a neighboring town, led him to say, "I might as well give it a crack. Plus the big office would be a nice bonus!"

So the next thing you know, fast forward past a few interviews, and "Mr. Roger Rookie" is announced as the new principal of Anywhere Middle School (AMS)!

Oh my goodness, what did I get myself into? Roger thought. *Being responsible for an entire school is a BIG DEAL, yet I'll do my homework and BE READY.*

Roger scratched down an "I'm a Principal Now To-Do" list on the new notepad he bought at the college bookstore. He was always writing notes to himself and drawing pictures. Kept him from having to remember everything in his head. Plus . . . he liked to doodle.

Let's see . . . a focus on learning, he pondered as he sketched.

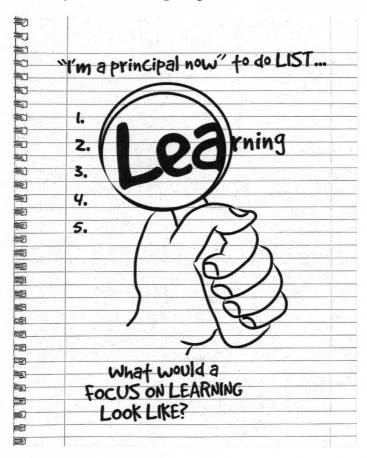

Roger imagined the first day of school, staff arriving, ready to follow his lead on a path toward better learning. Students would step up for the young, hip principal. Staff, too! And . . . after all, he had a master's degree. How hard could this be?

Roger did his best thinking late at night. With a bag of popcorn on hand, soft drink at the ready, and his favorite late night TV shows playing, he started imagining what his new role would entail.

I chose education to make a difference. This new gig is a way to have an even broader influence. Heck, I don't know much about Anywhere Middle School, but if you have seen one school, then you have seen them all, haven't you? I'll discover the secret to this leadership thing in no time. I'll whip that school into shape!

Yet Roger had not heard very good things about Anywhere Middle School, or Mr. Neverthere, the previous principal, for that matter. He rubbed his hands together, wrote down a few thoughts and ideas on his notepad, and anxiously thought of the teachers and students who were to report that fall.

Let's See Focus on Learning
QUICK!

What's the secret? The Path??
"here's thoughts"

- Start upbeat, with confidence
- Give a PEP talk!
- But my textbook says,

"First watch, wait to Act."
and "Don't rock the boat"
and "Avoid the potholes."

Hmmm
- fake it 'til you make it, Right?!?

ok, I'm ready.
LET'S DO IT!

FIRST FACULTY MEETING

As Roger reviewed his notes, he was excited and nervous for his first faculty meeting. It was the teachers' first day back from summer break, and the principal was expected "on duty" to meet his staff and fire up his troops! As he walked into the room for the meeting, his last thought was, *I am going to change Anywhere Middle School.*

Looking at the group of teachers before him, Roger introduced himself and shared a little about his background.

"I know you're all very excited to move this school forward!" he said, expecting thunderous applause, or at least a smattering. Not getting any, he said, "So don't hesitate to show me what you got!! We're going to reinvent this school's reputation!"

What Roger got instead, was a rousing round of "look."

Fumbling a bit, he then introduced Nellie Newcomer, the newest addition to the AMS faculty, and asked her to share a little bit about herself.

"Hi, I'm Nellie Newcomer, recent graduate from Over There Teachers College. I'm very excited to begin decorating my classroom and getting to know all of you. I hope to learn about how things work around here very quickly, so that I can get more involved and make a difference. It will be nice meeting you all."

Nellie seemed a little nervous when she talked but got through it okay. She did get embarrassed when someone in the back muttered, "That's who they hired over my nephew?!? I wonder who she's related to."

Roger chose to ignore the comment, proceeded through several management tasks, and read some rules from the handbook. He then shifted to school reform, as he had just read something about it in his last college class.

"A principal's job is to be an 'instructional leader', and thus I plan on visiting classrooms every day. I'm going to learn from the great work you're doing! Together, we are going to focus on learning and put Anywhere Middle School's name in lights!"

He then shared that Anywhere needed to do something about its test scores.

"Central Office had a meeting last week and said that everyone needs to increase the performance on the state exams, so we really need to make this a focus this year."

As Roger stood in front of the group with a big smile on his face, one teacher stood with hand on hip, bent finger in the air, long nose with eyeglasses affixed . . . Roger believed her name was Mildred Morose.

She said loudly, "Excuse me, but I didn't know we had a problem at Anywhere Middle School. I've been here over thirty years, and I think this is a pretty good school. And if we want to improve anything here, maybe somebody should do something about these students. I don't know how we can raise a test score with kids and parents who don't care. If it doesn't matter to them, then I don't see why it should matter to us. You can lead a horse to water . . . as they say . . ."

Roger looked around the room; several teachers nodded in agreement with Mildred Morose. He even thought he heard someone whisper, "Amen, sister!"

Roger Rookie turned a little red, but gathered his thoughts and said, "What I meant to say is that we will build on the great work that is already being done at AMS."

A couple of people in the back, near the door, snickered but did not comment.

After a short pause, Roger continued down his list. He noticed that as he was discussing attendance procedures, a handful of teachers were talking with each other somewhat loudly. He also saw a teacher knitting and two doing crossword puzzles or Sudokus. Roger ignored the distractions but felt very uncomfortable. By the end of the faculty meeting, Roger could not avoid the fact that only a handful of teachers still appeared to be listening to what he was saying.

Feeling awkward, Roger quickly ended the meeting.

Shortly after his meeting, Roger was in his office when he saw a teacher at his door wanting to speak with him. It was Judy Slacker, veteran teacher.

"Hello, Mr. Rookie, I'm Mrs. Slacker, and I would like to thank you, first of all, for such a short faculty meeting. The teachers at Anywhere have so much to do in preparing for our students; it is good to have a leader who understands this."

Roger felt good with the compliment yet a bit uneasy, as the short meeting was not his intent.

She went on, "As you have mentioned your role as our instructional leader, you must understand that young Nellie Newcomer needs a mentor. Always one willing to serve, in the best interests of children and commensurate compensation, I am volunteering my twenty seven years of experience to be Miss Newcomer's mentor."

Roger readied what was to be a *taken under advisement* response, when Judy continued, "I have already spoken with the other teachers in their departments, and they all agreed that it was only fair if I get the extra stipend to mentor Nellie. I have the most seniority."

Roger, smiling on the outside, tried to envision a diplomatic solution that would result in Judy's not mentoring Miss Newcomer. His mind raced. It did not take a rocket scientist to conclude that Judy did not appear to be "student-centered."

Nellie Newcomer's excellent interview and references indicated she was going to be a fantastic teacher, focused 100 percent on the children. Nellie was Roger's first hire, so he felt particularly responsible for ensuring that she got the support she was going to need in her first year.

"Mrs. Slacker . . . I just don't quite know where I want to go with this [searching for a way out, yet seeing none] . . . however, since you have made it a point to talk with others, and since we probably should begin providing some assistance to Nellie right away, why don't we give it a go."

"Good decision, Mr. Rookie; it is what we as a faculty would expect."

Roger turned and said, "When do you think you and Nellie might . . ."

Judy Slacker was already out the office door, en route to the teachers' lounge, passing Nellie Newcomer along the way without a word.

Nellie continued down a side hallway, learning her way around the building by trial and error.

Roger thought, *Not a bad idea . . . a quick lounge visit. I need to be in touch with my faculty.* He walked into the teachers' lounge to get a cup of coffee and found it interesting that a few teachers looked surprised to see the principal in the *teachers'* lounge.

Roger poured a cup of coffee and sat down next to Karl Chameleon. Karl was in his eighth year of teaching mathematics. Roger asked Karl how his summer break had been. Karl spoke quickly and told Roger a very long story about his vacation with his family to Mount Rushmore.

Nice enough guy, Roger thought. *Family man.*

As Roger was getting ready to make a comment, another teacher, La-Von Babble, asked Roger, "Mr. Rookie, given that my daycare provider cannot watch my children after school, would you have a problem if I left school early on Mondays, Wednesdays, and Fridays?"

Others listened with interest.

LaVon continued, "I can leave at the end of the last period, when students are leaving; but know that on those days, I'll come in early to make up the time. This is really the same arrangement that I had with Mr. Neverthere, yet I'm asking you as a courtesy, fully expecting that you will support your faculty with things such as this."

She concluded by noting that the arrangement worked out well in the past, calling it a "win/win."

Other teachers chimed in quickly, sharing that teachers work many evenings and weekends, and that leaving a little early on occasion was not a big deal.

Roger mumbled, "Let me give this some thought, Mrs. Babble," then got up and walked out of the room.

It was the end of the day. Roger looked up from his desk and noticed that Nellie Newcomer was standing at the door.

Nellie smiled and said, "I want to thank you again, Mr. Rookie, for giving me an opportunity as a teacher. I'm not going to let you down."

Roger responded, "Thank you, Nellie, that's nice to hear. Please know that if you need any help, do not hesitate to ask." He continued, "You will be interested to know that I have assigned Mrs. Slacker as your mentor."

Her face dimmed.

"I'm hoping that Judy will provide you with the necessary support you are going to need as a first-year teacher." Roger questioned whether he believed this statement, yet tried not to let it show.

PARENT MEETING

On the second day of Anywhere's back-to-school workshop, Roger had a meeting scheduled with the Johnson family. They had two students attending AMS. It didn't take long in the meeting to learn that the family was upset with the school secretary.

Anywhere Middle School had two secretaries in the main office. The primary secretary was Trudy Savage. Beyond the imposing, deeply riveted symmetry of her furrowed unibrow, Trudy Savage's entire visage resembled that of a praying mantis, poised to pounce and paralyze victims with a barb of her sharp tongue and devour their necks quickly while leaving their lifeless corpses for grazing (and of course, deterrence).

Trudy Savage was well known throughout the community for her lack of people skills and overall negative attitude. The comments she would often make were unbelievable! Parents routinely reported being treated poorly and avoided Trudy Savage whenever possible.

She could often be heard saying, "Last time I looked in the mirror, I was the one running this office," and "There's something to be said for apples and trees, don't you think?"

She wasn't too fond of students, or adults for that matter.

The other secretary, Kris Bliss, was friendly and helpful. And . . . the "most busy."

Teachers and parents quickly learned that Kris was the secretary to have all conversations with in the office. She was the one who helped the folks and considered everyone at Anywhere Middle School her extended family. Kris had pictures of her family adorning her office area along with scented candles and thank-you notes of appreciation.

Trudy Savage's desk calendar read, "Take a number . . . Better yet, DEAL WITH IT Yourself!!"

Roger continued his conversation with the Johnson family.

According to Mrs. Johnson, Trudy Savage had told her, "If you can't afford the registration fees, you need to think about getting a job to support your children appropriately. You don't want this cycle to repeat itself, do you!?!"

Roger was shocked by what the Johnsons were sharing. He knew Mrs. Savage lacked interpersonal skills, but this comment was way out-of-bounds.

I wonder if I should ask Mrs. Savage to join us in the meeting to present her side of the story, Roger pondered. *Probably not, her presence would only make things worse.*

Roger said, "I'm so very sorry you were treated this way. It does not represent how we should be partnering with our families at Anywhere

Middle School. Please know that I will definitely investigate your concerns."

The Johnsons thanked Roger Rookie for meeting with them and listening to their issues.

Roger never met with Trudy Savage about the Johnsons' complaint; he chose to avoid the problem.

Didn't want his head devoured.

READING DEPARTMENT MEETING

The reading department was excited to meet with Roger Rookie. The department consisted of seven teachers and, unlike some of the other AMS departments, they worked well together.

Sandy Starr, department head, had been trying to arrange a meeting between her department and Roger Rookie since his first day on the job, but he kept postponing the meeting. It was now a month or so into the school year. Mrs. Starr finally pinned him down.

Sandy Starr had a reputation for being an outstanding teacher. Roger had reviewed her student achievement data. It was significantly higher than that of almost all other teachers at AMS. Mrs. Starr opened the meeting with introductions and announcements.

She then said for the benefit of Roger, "Our department had been working for over a year on how to improve the reading skills of students who were multiple years below grade level. Unlike the elementary, Anywhere Middle School did not have a program specific to its struggling readers. That was until we learned about a research-based reading program designed specifically for secondary students."

Several schools, Mrs. Starr reported, had implemented the program and had significant increases in student achievement data.

"We as reading teachers are excited, as we feel like we have finally discovered a reading program that is perfect for AMS. At this time, we would like to share some of the details with you, Mr. Rookie, on why we feel this way."

As the teachers took turns describing the specifics of the program, Roger Rookie quietly listened. He asked a few clarifying questions but did not appear too interested in learning about the program. He was thinking of Trudy Savage, the Johnsons, and the first staff meeting. Finally, after the department finished its presentation, Sandy Starr asked, "Mr. Rookie, what are your thoughts on implementing the program at AMS?"

"It brings with it a number of factors to consider, yet it is worthy of a closer look," said Mr. Rookie, thanking the reading department for their hard work and noting that he would consider their request.

Hmmm, that's a positive step. Those folks seem to be focused on learning, he thought as he walked back to his office. *Maybe the secret to better learning at Anywhere Middle School is just looking, listening, not rocking the boat, and letting faculty come up with better plans for instruction,* he mulled.

Roger wasn't sure how Central Office would respond to the reading program idea because he got a sense they were not interested in doing things that would increase spending.

I'm not sure I want to go down that road with my superintendent right now, he thought. *Although our scores in reading really do need to improve, I'm not sure I can spend any money. Better hold off. Better not make waves.*

2

ROGER ROOKIE'S FIRST MAKEOVER: THE HIBERNATOR

A week later, Roger was working in his office when he heard Trudy Savage yell, "Come to me, 'My Pretty,' I've been waiting to see you!"

Trudy then launched into Nellie Newcomer for "pilfering" extra markers from the storeroom. Nellie was horrified. She had not yet been told of the "Trudy rules." Taking supplies without her approval was the Number One Unwritten Rule a teacher did not break.

"Do you mean to tell me, young thing, given the fact that you purportedly received an education prior to your arrival, that they didn't teach you in 'How-to-Be-a-Teacher School' to get permission before taking things that aren't yours? We teach THAT to children in kindergarten!!"

Before Nellie had a chance to apologize, Trudy Savage began pointing her finger, yelling that taking supplies without proper authorization was unprofessional and that Mr. Rookie would be notified promptly.

Nellie almost started crying.

A parent in the office quietly walked out.

Boys sent to the office paced outside, afraid to go in, yet equally afraid of Mrs. Savage's wrath if they didn't enter to *Sit in Shame*, as she required.

Roger heard everything but did not know what to do, so he quietly moved toward his office door, trying not to be heard, and then closed it, sitting back down at his desk.

He hesitated and thought to himself, *Well, Trudy IS Trudy. Probably best to let her "regulate." She's keeping more work off my desk by setting the tone. And I need to spend my time finding the secret to this learning thing. She's probably one to 'Never Smile 'til November.' Though I do hope it will be November soon.*

Nellie Newcomer left the office upset. Roger rubbed his neck uncomfortably and opened his e-mail, thinking of something that a principal would send to his staff to help increase the focus on learning.

Nellie decided she needed to visit with her mentor, Judy Slacker, for support.

Judy, meanwhile, was in her room talking with her friend, Mildred Morose. "You know, Mildred, the one thing I always say about the start of a new school year . . . it's a great feeling, until those darn kids arrive."

"Tell me about it! I don't know if it's too much television or family trees without branches, but something's sure wrong with these children nowadays!"

They both cackled.

When Nellie walked in, they continued talking, knowing full well she was there. Nellie couldn't believe what they were saying about students, and even some of the other adults in the building.

Finally, after several minutes, Judy Slacker, with an *"And, what do you want?"* look, asked Nellie Newcomer what was so important that couldn't possibly wait to be shared until the next lunch period in the lounge.

"Mrs. Savage just yelled at me in the office for taking supplies. She did this in front of everyone, and I feel as low as a carpet fiber. I hope that I'm not in trouble with Mr. Rookie," she said. "Mrs. Savage threatened to turn me in to him."

Judy Slacker and Mildred Morose laughed.

"Oh, come ON, Dearie," said Mildred. "Everyone knows you don't just take things from Trudy Savage's office. You're lucky she didn't chop off your hand at the knuckle or chew on your neck."

"Haven't you learned the *'Anywhere Way'* yet, little lady?!?" asked Judy. "C'mon newbie . . . toughen up. You're in big girl school now."

As they continued to laugh, Nellie Newcomer left the classroom and walked back to her room feeling embarrassed and lonely.

THE BULLIES

Roger Rookie discovered in his first few weeks that the Anywhere Middle School staff had a pecking order. He privately referred to the dominant group of teachers as The Bullies, as he had heard of their existence prior to his arrival.

The Bullies had a few main members: Mildred Morose, Judy Slacker, and LaVon Babble. Edgar Sleeper seemed to hang with them quite a bit but didn't say much. He was sort of like their lap dog.

Mildred was the ringleader. She was one of the most veteran teachers in the district and was not afraid to engage in conflict with anybody, including the principal, which Roger found out the hard way at his first faculty meeting.

Mildred Morose was loud, dominating, and confrontational. She walked a bit crooked. A select group of students were loyal to her, almost cult-like; they were her minions and treated others as outcasts. In short, they were learning from her. What was disappointing to Roger was that the staff did not seem upset by Mildred's behavior. He could not understand why they tolerated her dominance and didn't stand up to her.

Judy Slacker was also a veteran teacher and almost as bad as Mildred. She was pretty negative as well and was the last teacher you would want your own child to have. Students did not worship her, however, as the select group worshiped Mildred. They did not mind having Mrs. Slacker for a teacher either, as routine in her classroom was fairly predictable. Day after day . . . read the text, do worksheets, turn things in . . . repeat the process . . . while Mrs. Slacker was on her computer. Kids could be invisible in Mrs. Slacker's class.

LaVon Babble had been at AMS about ten years and was not as bad as Mildred and Judy. She was always at their side. Mostly, she did personal business during school hours: online shopping, telephone calls, and even paying her bills while kids read and did worksheets. She was in the hallways with The Bullies after each class bell rang, urging students to get to class, yet without proceeding to her own.

Trading insider jokes was more the rule than the exception. The Bullies always ate together at the same lounge table and carried a short list of student mishaps to share with others, at the students' expense. They had unflattering nicknames for everyone, even each other.

Despite some of the major problems at AMS, The Bullies appeared to like how the school was operating. At least they liked how it was running FOR THEM. Others were vying for their affection. Rumor had it that one time a few years back, Edgar Sleeper was sitting in the teachers' lounge with his feet up on the table when Mr. Neverthere stopped by his classroom for a formal classroom evaluation. Not finding Edgar in his class, yet finding his students playing cards, Mr. Neverthere stormed out and down the hall.

Upon discovering Edgar in the lounge, Mr. Neverthere stated, "Edgar, I was just in your classroom!"

Edgar responded, "Well, boss . . . is everything goin' OK?"

The Bullies had big fun with that one.

Edgar Sleeper was awarded their merit badge that day. Karl Chameleon now tried for it every so often. The role didn't fit him as well, but, more and more, he was trying it on for size.

Deep down, Roger was actually a bit afraid of Mildred Morose. He hated the fact that he allowed her to have power, but the truth was, she was scary.

Turning to his in-box, Roger had a big smile on his face as he reread the congratulatory e-mail from Central Office:

> Dear Principal Rookie: On behalf of the superintendent and Central Office leadership team, we would like to commend you for getting your attendance reports turned in before any other principal in the district. Your proactivity in meeting our deadlines helps further the cause for school improvement and district-wide accountability.

In little time, Roger had established a reputation with Central Office for responding to its requests very quickly. Roger took great pride in making sure his business was conducted efficiently and on time. This required him to spend a lot of time in his office, sometimes with the door closed.

Roger took out his notebook and jotted down a few things that he felt were keeping him on track.

STAYIN' ON TRACK

- Any good business must run like a machine.
- Keeping the gears running smoothly is key.
- Avoiding bumps in production is Principal's job.
- That'll probably HELP LEARNING.
- No side roads, no detours
- Gotta keep the train on the tracks ⫟⫟⫟⫟⟶
- No time to lay down new tracks.
- Keep the Train A-Movin'.
- That's probably the SECRET!

Nellie Newcomer grabbed her sack lunch and headed to the teachers' lounge. As she walked in, she heard Mildred Morose ask, "Has anybody seen our fearless principal in the last two weeks? It must be nice to earn a fat check and sit in your office all day playing solitaire. Trudy Savage told me she makes most of the decisions and does it for one-third the pay."

Laughter.

Nellie felt uncomfortable.

Karl Chameleon mentioned, "Hey, folks, I have a friend who teaches at Central Middle School. Last week they scheduled a staff meeting at someone's house for a fall get-together. Guess they even had a barbecue! Wonder why Rookie never schedules any fun activities for our staff? We do a lot of great things here, and nobody ever recognizes what we do."

Judy Slacker then took her turn to lambaste Roger Rookie. "You're not going to believe that, over two weeks ago, I asked for a parking spot next to the building because I was having problems with my foot—you all know of that plantar wart, bunion fiasco that I've been dealing with, along with that rash. Well, anyway . . . Rookie told me he would have to get back to me. Didn't happen! Hasn't happened! I think the reason our boy toy hides in his office all day is so he doesn't have to face me. If I don't get an answer soon, I'm going to sic Mildred on him. I don't think he wants any part of her."

Laughter.

Mildred Morose grinned a sinister grin.

The entire lounge laughed, except for one person.

Nellie Newcomer did not think what they were saying was funny and thought that the comments were completely disrespectful. However, she too had misgivings about the leadership of Roger Rookie.

When Roger Rookie hired her, he told her he would be in her classroom to provide her with support. However, he had not been in her classroom since the first week of school. That was for only a minute to tell her about some paperwork that needed to be turned in.

Nellie hated the way she felt in the teachers' lounge. As she looked around, it dawned on her who was in the lounge: Mildred Morose, Judy Slacker, Karl Chameleon, Edgar Sleeper, LaVon Babble, and a handful of others. However, Nellie also noticed who wasn't in the lounge.

In fact, there were some teachers she never saw in the teachers' lounge, like Sandy Starr. Nellie decided this would be her last trip to the lounge and that she needed to pay Sandy Starr a visit.

WHAT SUPERSTARS DO

Sandy Starr was displaying student work on a wall when Nellie Newcomer knocked on her door. "Come in, please; it's so nice to see you, Nellie," Sandy smiled as she invited Nellie into her classroom.

Sandy apologized to Nellie for not stopping by her room in the past couple of weeks. She had, however, made a point to check in on Nellie each of the first weeks of school, but had gotten busy and had not made it down to her room in recent weeks.

Nellie told her, "I so very much appreciate the support you have given me here at Anywhere, and I understand that you are busy with your own students."

Nellie then shared the details of her trip to the teachers' lounge and the comments that were made about Principal Rookie. As Nellie described the group and their behavior, Sandy just listened and nodded occasionally. She looked concerned and disappointed, but not overly surprised.

Then Nellie asked, "Why don't we ever see you in the teachers' lounge?"

Sandy Starr responded, "Did you know I used to teach at another school? In the last school district I worked in, I actually spent time in the teachers' lounge. I would go there during prep time or sometimes eat lunch with other staff members and the principal."

"At that school, the culture was completely different from AMS. Teachers were friendly, supportive and helpful. The principal had a great relationship with the staff, and I really felt like we were a team. Since that was my first job, I thought all schools operated that way."

She continued, "However, when my husband was transferred to this area five years ago and I was hired at AMS, I soon discovered that AMS was quite different. In my first year at AMS, when I would go to the teachers' lounge, the teachers rarely talked about students, but when they did, it was in a very negative manner and they frequently complained about the administration. So, four and half years ago, I quit going to the lounge."

Nellie brought up Roger Rookie. She told Mrs. Starr, "I am not at all trying to be negative or critical of Mr. Rookie, but I never see him, and he assigned Mrs. Slacker as my mentor. I never see her either."

Sandy Starr shook her head empathetically. She agreed that Nellie deserved more support. "I heard about the way Mrs. Savage treated you in the office, and I felt so bad for you. I don't know why she is allowed to treat people the way she does; it makes our whole school look bad."

"I feel like she's going to pounce on me and chew my head off my shoulders," said Nellie. "I don't think she likes me."

Sandy continued, "Mr. Rookie is only in his first couple of months as a principal, and hopefully he will be able to get things turned around at AMS. As for Mrs. Savage, Nellie . . . well, that's a bit more complicated."

Sandy Starr then suggested to Nellie that she join a small group of teachers that occasionally gets together in a coffee klatch or meets in a classroom for lunch to socialize and support each other. "Our next meeting is Friday morning in my room at 7:00. You do not need to bring anything; just tell me what you like to drink in the morning and I will take care of it."

Nellie smiled and gladly accepted Sandy Starr's invitation. Nellie thanked her and told her she had really needed this talk.

As Roger entered the building with his morning coffee in hand, he noticed Karl Chameleon meeting with The Bullies in Mildred Morose's classroom. He recalled other times in the past couple of weeks when he had seen Karl hanging out with The Bullies.

Roger shook his head in amazement that somebody would want to join a negative group like them. As he walked toward his office, he heard loud laughter coming from The Bullies. *They are really having a world of a good time*, he thought.

He was a bit envious that he hadn't laughed like that since becoming principal, yet he knew deep down that theirs was almost certainly at someone else's expense.

SECOND FACULTY MEETING

Roger waited as long as he could, but he had to have another faculty meeting, primarily because his superintendent had directed all building principals to provide meeting minutes to his office quarterly. There were also simply too many things the staff needed to discuss, and his twenty-five to thirty e-mails per day couldn't handle everything that needed discussion. So, he e-mailed the staff and announced the faculty meeting.

As Roger walked into the meeting, his last thought was, *I hope nobody embarrasses me.*

The beginning of the meeting went well. Roger was actually able to get through all of his agenda items without any trouble. He asked if there were any questions or comments before they adjourned. Looking around the room, he saw that Nellie Newcomer had her hand up.

"Yes, Nellie, you have something to share with us?"

Nellie cleared her throat and then said sheepishly, "Well, at a recent meeting in Mrs. Starr's room, we discussed strategies to help our students with homework. Some of our students do not get a lot of support at home, so we were wondering if we could take turns and start an after-school tutoring program?"

The first thing Roger noticed was that Sandy Starr and a handful of other teachers immediately dropped their heads.

Mildred Morose wasted no time, standing abruptly and loudly sharing, "As we are all concerned with the children, we are also concerned with ourselves as a faculty. The union has worked too hard over the years to get teachers properly compensated for all of the extras that they do on a weekly basis, and there is no way I am going to provide free teaching, but of course . . . I cannot control what others of you do with your time."

She added with a swing of her elongated finger, "Be careful that what you are doing will not set precedent because, if it does, you'll find yourselves doing it for the rest of your career. Oh, and as this may be helpful in your decision making, other naïve teachers and principals have tried tutoring in the past. It did not work then, and it will not work now, as what we seek to correct is more a parental supervision issue than it is an educational issue."

Roger Rookie thanked Mildred Morose for her comment and told Nellie he would consider it. Nellie looked around and realized that apparently she had done something wrong. The *Anywhere Way* was talking to her, albeit softly. As part of this, the staff was already conditioned to know that Roger's comment meant that he was **not** going to consider it.

THE PRINCIPAL SURVEY

School had been in session for three months, so Roger Rookie decided it would help him in his professional growth if he surveyed the staff. He knew he was doing a great job with helping the school get organized. In a few short months, he had already updated several school documents, including the strategic plan, the annual report, and the student handbook.

However, Roger knew there were areas in which he could improve.
So he e-mailed every staff member a link to an online survey and asked
the staff to take five minutes to complete it.

I can't wait to hear what they have to say, he thought. *I'll bet I'm a
bit light in knowledge of building and grounds planning, as I have not
held too many work sessions on these subjects, as of yet.*

It took a few reminders, but after a couple of days, all staff members
had completed the survey. Roger sat down at his desk and began reviewing the survey results.

He was stunned. He knew that, with an anonymous survey, some staff
members might take the opportunity to make critical comments, but the
entire staff rated him poorly in almost every category.

Worse, the comments about his lack of leadership were scathing—
not only in building management, but also in his instructional leadership and facilitating community resources. Comment after comment
complained about his lack of visibility. He wrote down those of more
concern in his notebook for later thought.

From my (Job) PERFORMANCE Survey

"Never see the Principal, except during Lunch Duty"

"Too many closed doors not enough conversations"

"Would like a classroom visit from time to time"

"Wondering what he's doing in his office all the time"

"Never thought I'd work for a celebrity, THE INVISIBLE MAN"

"Who's Roger Rookie?"

Multiple teachers referenced his comment in August about visiting
classrooms, and indicated that he had not followed through. School climate was another prominent theme mentioned in the survey. The staff
clearly felt that school climate was poor. He jotted down some of these
comments as well.

Roger Rookie was speechless. He closed his notebook, tossed his pen, rubbed his head, and then took the weekend to reflect on the survey's results. After being defensive initially, Roger eventually admitted to himself that the main themes from the survey, and many of the comments, were accurate.

Sitting with his favorite popcorn and soda in hand watching late-night TV, Roger came to terms with the fact that he had been focusing on the wrong priorities to make AMS a great school.

I've been a Hibernator, Roger concluded. *I have been avoiding what I need to do as a leader to begin creating a better focus on learning.*

With 20/20 hindsight, he scribbled a few ideas to try and thought, *Come Monday, things are going to change at Anywhere Middle School.*

TEACHERS' LOUNGE

"You know how many Rookies it takes to hold a staff meeting?" said Karl Chameleon to his eager audience. "One to e-mail the agenda, another to stand publicly and endure Mildred's spanking machine, and a final one to 'take things under advisement' so that he can return to his office and NOT make a decision."

Everyone laughed.

"Hey . . . c'mon Chameleon, you're starting to sound like Edgar Sleeper, who's really been on this *Rookie . . . the 'Son Neverthere Never Had'* thing," said Judy Slacker. "Give Rookie a break, the poor thing. He's tuckered out after resting all day in his big chair reading and sending those tiresome e-mails."

Judy continued, "Imagine how difficult it must be to lug around his large pay increase that he received last summer. Almost as difficult as your heavy lifting, Chameleon, at the golf course."

"Yeah . . . OK, OK . . . those new oversized drivers are getting a bit tiring to lug around in that golf cart," Karl said with a smirk.

"Hey . . . as far as I'm concerned, there are 365 days in a school year," said Judy Slacker, "and if I'm going to be expected to work more than half of them, I'll be more than happy to enjoy the money that comes along with it [she paused and smiled] . . . or file a grievance and give Rookie a real education about what it's like to run a building."

Laughter again.

"Hey, Judy, what are you teaching that new girl you're mentoring?" asked Mildred Morose.

"Well, just like boot camp—you gotta let the drill sergeant have at her," Judy Slacker replied. "Yep, she's been to Trudy's whipping post a few times so far."

"How's that going for the girl?" someone asked.

"No visible lacerations . . . just a few internal injuries. It's good for her . . . plus a bit fun to watch. We've all been there!"

"Next, once Rookie gives her about three or four more false promises, we'll let her know how things really work around here."

Mildred added, "I imagine at this point, Sandy Starr is filling her full of a bunch of hearts and smiles. That'll get old. She's new . . . wet behind the ears. She'll come around and realize who runs this show. You losers better keep that seat over there warm for her."

Laughter again.

THE COFFEE KLATCH

"How have things wrapped up this quarter, Nellie?" inquired Sandy Starr.

"Well, I think things are going in the right direction, Mrs. Starr, but to be quite frank, I'm still a bit unsure if I'm on track with the students. The pacing guide and curriculum map help to a certain degree, but what I really need is a bit more time with Mr. Rookie, to see if things are really on track," said Nellie.

"Give him a bit more time, Nellie," Sandy Starr said with reassurance. "He's had a very busy start in his first year as a principal. The one thing I have learned in my many years of teaching is that we may not know the pressures that others face in their jobs. Regarding his unavailability, I am hoping that this too shall pass."

"I try to do that. What I'm concerned about, however, is not simply the fact that I will be evaluated based on my students' performance, but unless I make a positive difference in their lives, my students will not be ready for high school and college. It's one thing to say that I can wait a year or two for good guidance and direction, but my students need good guidance and direction right now. That's my biggest worry."

"It is a valid worry to have, Nellie. I'll continue helping any way that I can. Let us hope things improve sooner, rather than later. For the most part, I'll be in my classroom, keeping out of the line of fire and doing what I can to help my students. Feel free to visit at anytime."

ROGER ROOKIE'S DEEP THOUGHTS

THE HIBERNATOR'S EFFECTS ON STAFF...

SUPERSTARS
- Do not get approval and reinforcement
- Miss interacting with leader
- Feel like they are on an island

FENCESITTERS
- Will blame things in your absence
- Feel uncomfortable making decisions
- Look for leadership in all the wrong places

BULLIES
- Become very powerful
- Complain about your hiding, but actually like it
- Fill the "Leadership Void"

THE HIBERNATOR
continued...

THE LEADER FEELS
- Indecisive
- Afraid
- Powerless

UNINTENDED CONSEQUENCES
- Negative people gain power
- Good people lose confidence
- Leader is unaware of what is happening in the school

ROGER ROOKIE'S NEXT MAKEOVER: THE GLAD-HANDER

Roger scheduled a faculty meeting for Monday morning at 7:30. He was determined to learn from the survey results. As Roger walked into the faculty meeting, his last thought was, *I am going to change the climate in this building. That'll help learning! I just know I'm on to something. I'll find that path! Let the secret be revealed!!*

As teachers started filing in, they were surprised to see an assortment of bagels, muffins, orange juice, and coffee. Roger began the meeting by thanking the staff for taking the time to complete his survey.

Roger then said, "I want to apologize. The first quarter of the school year I have been busy, but I chose to focus my energy on the wrong things. I was avoiding some things I should have focused more on. I need to focus more on you all. School climate is *NUMERO UNO* in importance, as I've learned from you all. Beginning today, I am committed to visiting classrooms and recognizing our students and staff for the great things you do. We are going to start having some fun around here."

Immediately, Nellie Newcomer, Sandy Starr, and others looked uncomfortable.

The Bullies appeared ready to complain, but to Roger's pleasant surprise, they did not say anything; they just kept filling their faces with treats and talking with one another. Roger finished the meeting by thanking the staff for their hard work.

Roger thought to himself, *Man, when I look in the mirror, I am looking at one smart cat!! If the teachers have food in their mouths, it's tough for them to complain. It may cost me a little scratch, but Sam's Club is going to be my new best friend. I'm buying in bulk!*

For the first two weeks after the meeting, Roger Rookie kept his word and visited classrooms every day. He was surprised to learn how good some of the AMS teachers were. Some of their lessons were a bit lacking in delivery, but with a little help, these teachers could be really good. And, he saw a couple of classrooms where teachers were consistently performing below standards. Roger knew he would never put his own children in those classrooms . . . well, when he had children anyway. First things first . . .

Roger knew as well that he needed to start developing positive relationships with students and parents. Although an e-mail or a form letter would have been more efficient, Roger instead spent time in the evening writing personal notes to students for improving their grades or behavior.

I've got to start connecting with each and every student and family, he decided. *I'll just know the secret to improved learning is taking care of people!*

He wrote note after note to staff members when he saw creative lessons in their classrooms. Roger made a point not to write the same note to every teacher.

I've got to make sure that each note is unique so that I am praising them for specific actions, Roger thought to himself.

Roger also sent notes to parents acknowledging their child's improvement or their support of the school. In doing so, he was amazed at how busy he was. Since he started visiting classrooms and recognizing people for positive performance or behavior, he liked his job more.

SEMINAR PROBLEM

One day after school, Roger returned to his office and saw a handful of teachers waiting for him. He took one look at the faces of the group and knew he was in trouble.

Oh, no . . . Mildred Morose and Judy Slacker. This isn't going to be a party!

This group of teachers had already distinguished themselves by finding innovative ways to spend **less** time with students.

Would that be what this impromptu meeting was all about? He wondered.

Roger welcomed the group, exchanged a few pleasantries, and asked the teachers what they wished to discuss.

Mildred Morose responded, "Mr. Rookie, our representative group of faculty would like to discuss Seminar, our school's advisor/advisee time."

Roger wondered who they actually represented, but cautioned himself against going this route.

She continued, "As you know, Seminar was extended five minutes by your predecessor, Mr. Neverthere, without any input from teachers. What I am sure he did not realize is that our lunch break has been reduced from thirty-five to thirty minutes. To compound the problem, this is the worst behaved bunch of malcontents we have ever had at Anywhere. We need as much recuperation time as anybody. Trudy Savage warned us of this after meeting their parents at summer registration."

Judy Slacker added, "Might a better approach be that paraprofessionals would cover lunch? In doing so, Seminar could revert to being five fewer minutes?"

Roger was surprised that five minutes of lunchtime was an issue.

Ned Neverthere had told Roger when he first arrived that Seminar had been implemented to help students build a relationship with the faculty during their years at AMS. It was also a structured setting that helped students stay organized with their homework.

Roger thought, *I remember Mr. Neverthere saying also that several teachers, his superstar teachers, had complained that they could use more Seminar time to help students, so he added another five minutes.*

Roger didn't share this with the group.

Roger assured the group that he would try to find a solution. "Thank you, Mr. Rookie," said Mildred Morose on behalf of the group. "We trust you will do the right thing."

They left for the teachers' lounge.

Roger thought about the group's request and, at the same time, mulled over his charge to improve a focus on learning at Anywhere Middle School.

While revisiting his old *How to Be a Good School Principal* textbooks late at night, with popcorn and soda pop as usual, Roger began jotting down some notes on what a focus on learning would look like. He noted,

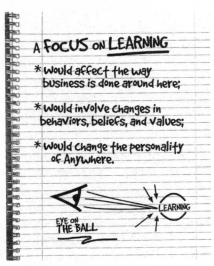

He studied his notes over and over and scratched out a few drawings of flowcharts and other things that would potentially impact a focus on learning. He reflected on the first quarter and how he didn't come out of his office much. Roger thought best when he doodled . . . and ate.

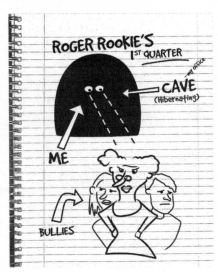

Roger pondered, *During the first quarter, I certainly got to know the way business was done around here, and I didn't like it. If behaviors and beliefs were any indication, I can see why my superintendent wants things changed. Too bad I spent nine weeks accepting things as they were. As principal, I gotta get something done.*

His thoughts wandered to Nellie. *Not sure who is helping Nellie, if anyone, but I feel bad that I assigned Judy Slacker as her mentor. Knew THAT was wrong in the first place. Stupid move! Back to my marching orders . . . just how can I move learning in a direction I want it to go?*

Roger thought of the initial success in his newfound overtures at building better relationships. He remembered the old adage, *The way to a person's heart is through his or her appetite.*

He surmised, *I just need to keep this ship sailing on the climate thing. If I make it my mission to take care of the needs of PEOPLE, each and every day, folks will love coming to work, because they'll feel good. This'll motivate them to do the right thing by kids, won't it?*

He then continued drawing and munching.

Yep, same to 'em but more of it. CLIMATE. It's the path! I'll do my darnedest to have the best school climate ever! If people LOVE working for me, and if they actually like me, then I'll bet we start making an impact on this learning thing.

If people are happier, aren't they more productive? That'll take care of the test scores. Boy, wouldn't that make my superintendent happy!?! Carol Charming would even write about it. I'd be a hero.

Roger Rookie doubled down on climate and, to be sure, climate was improving.

Writing positive notes continued, as did classroom walkthroughs and observations. Sure, all this attention to people gave him longer hours at work once everyone went home. Yet he was able to take some things home and work over snacks and late-night television, so things weren't all that bad.

With the climate slowly beginning to improve in the school, Roger Rookie did not want the Seminar issue to upset staff. It appeared that nobody liked former principal Ned Neverthere and Roger was determined to get the staff to like Roger Rookie much better.

Roger thought, *This is a tough group to win over; maybe if I "give" on this issue, then the staff might give me a break on something later, especially if I'm THEIR principal.*

Roger announced that henceforth Seminar would be reduced by five minutes. A couple of the teachers personally thanked Roger for respecting them and finding such a great solution. They then headed to the teachers' lounge.

Roger made a commitment to have regular meetings with new staff members.

He scheduled a meeting with Nellie to see how her first year was going. Nellie's excitement and love of teaching were evident as she described how lucky and honored she felt to be teaching at AMS. Roger probed a little deeper, and Nellie began sharing some struggles she was having with a few students. When Roger heard the students' names he was not surprised, as those students were challenges for almost the entire staff.

Roger asked Nellie, "How have your conversations been going between you and your mentor, Judy Slacker?"

He noticed immediately that Nellie had an awkward look on her face.

She told Roger, "Unfortunately, I have only met with Mrs. Slacker once—during the August workshop before school had started."

"Oh . . . that's not good, Nellie," Roger said. "I'll speak with Mrs. Slacker and encourage her to schedule biweekly meetings with you. I hope that this will allow her to serve as a better resource for you, Nellie."

Roger finished up the meeting and walked out, knowing his decision to allow Judy Slacker to be anyone's mentor was a mistake. He felt like a heel and knew he should meet with Judy and be specific about her role as a mentor.

Roger Rookie never met with Judy Slacker.

Instead, he sent the following e-mail to the entire staff:

Faculty colleagues:

Thank you for your efforts in serving students thus far this year. As a gentle reminder to all, will you please take some of your valuable time and ensure that every so often you stop by the classrooms of our newer staff members to offer them support, advice, and encouragement valued by members of our school family. I trust all is well with you and that you will support our new faculty in their launch of professional careers.

Warm regards,

Mr. Rookie

"Warm regards?!? School family?!? HAAHH!!" said Judy Slacker, sitting beside Edgar Sleeper, Mildred Morose, and Karl Chameleon in the faculty lounge.

"Gag me with the pointed end of a hot charcoal poker!! Do you think we're doing these newbies any favors by coddling them with group hugs? We'll leave that to Sandy Starr."

"If anything, they need to toughen up a bit," said Edgar.

"A good dose of 'tough love' is probably better for them, 'cause if they steel their resolve quick, they'll be much better off in the long run. These kids aren't getting any easier to educate . . . and don't even get me started on the parents!!"

Karl Chameleon nodded in agreement.

"I deleted the e-mail as soon as I saw the source," said Mildred Morose. "I have no time for Rookie-isms . . . other things need my attention, like my knitting. What did it say?"

Laughter.

The only people that were influenced by Roger Rookie's e-mail were the most effective teachers. Although they had done a great job of helping new staff, they felt guilty for not doing more. It certainly did not change behavior with those who needed it changed. It certainly didn't help Nellie, that's for sure.

As part of his personal improvement plan that he reported to his superintendent, Roger Rookie had determined the school needed monthly faculty meetings to stay organized. He also started putting out the agenda to all staff members several days prior to the meeting and asking staff to add any items to the agenda that they wished to discuss.

Roger didn't care who offered up items or how many there were, as his new strategy of an "All You Can Eat Breakfast Buffet" was significantly reducing the number of complaints at meetings. Yet it seemed that the direction of conversation was getting away from him.

His new first agenda item at the faculty meetings was "Positive Comments."

Roger had gotten in the habit of using specific praise to point out extraordinary performance by teachers and anonymous praise (sometimes made up) about observing a "teacher" doing something remarkable with students.

He said, "Last week, I had the opportunity to walk by a classroom and spent a few minutes with rapt attention to the high interest and engagement of students in hearing how their academic learning was to make a difference in their lives. To have faculty members with such a command of their subject matter and the best interest of students is quite humbling, for sure. Thank you for that opportunity as your leader!"

He saw Karl Chameleon smile, look at Edgar Sleeper, and then point to himself. Edgar shook his head in friendly banter and pointed back at himself. Roger loved using anonymous praise because every time he used it, he could just tell that several teachers thought he was specifically talking about them.

Roger hoped that the combination of free food and positive comments would put teachers in a good mood so that he could have a meeting without controversy.

The meeting started well. Roger was able to get through most of the agenda with few questions or comments. With the finish line in sight, he was about to adjourn the meeting when he looked up and saw Mildred Morose trying to catch his eye.

Roger wondered why Mildred was actually behaving civilly and raising her hand, when she normally just rudely interrupted him.

Reluctantly, Roger said, "Yes, Mrs. Morose, what is on your mind?"

Mildred stood up, cleared her throat and, in a completely fake voice that she must have thought made her sound like a pleasant person, asked, "Could we please have conversation on why the school couldn't use paraprofessionals to cover the before-school duty?"

She continued, before Roger responded, positioning herself upright for greater visibility, "As you know, Mr. Rookie, we teachers serve a fifteen-minute, six-week supervision of the commons area prior to students being dismissed to their first-hour class. You, of all people, know how big our class sizes are this year. If we want any chance of raising test scores, which seems to be so important to Central Office, we need more time to prepare for this group of monsters."

The "monsters" comment got a laugh out of the usual cast of malcontents.

Edgar Sleeper then jumped into the fracas. "Mr. Rookie, the staff is still so grateful to you for using paraprofessionals to cover the lunch line, wouldn't it make sense to also use paraprofessionals to cover the before-school duty? We took a poll and have found that most faculty would concur."

A poll, Roger thought. *I'm not a fan of these polls.*

Judy Slacker and LaVon Babble were nodding in agreement, and Roger noticed several others joining them. As Roger looked around the room, he also noticed that some of his best teachers could not look him in the eyes; they had their heads down.

Roger did not know what to do. He didn't want conflict or pushback, so he told the group he would consider their request. *I wonder if more paraprofessional supervision would help their mood and the school climate*, he pondered?

PHONING A FRIEND

Roger phoned a friend. He called his old college buddy, Joel Gerrymander, who was in his third year as a principal/athletic director.

Truth be told, Roger thought, *this guy plays a bit fast and loose with his job, but he's a friend who will surely give me ten minutes of conversation and a straight answer, like it or not.*

Joel answered his call enthusiastically, "Dude . . . what's happening! I hear you got the big chair now. Oh . . . just one second, text message INCOMING!"

Telephone on his shoulder, Joel Gerrymander's thumbs worked like lightning to answer the text.

"OK, Rog . . . I'm back. WhazzzzUP!"

"Great to hear your voice, Joel. Yes, I took over for Ned Neverthere and have my superintendent breathing down my neck to make our school more focused on learning. You know, Joel, I have a situation, if you don't mind taking just a few minutes."

"Of course not . . . Shoot!" said Joel with interest.

Roger shared his faculty meeting concern about The Bullies. Joel listened as best he could while shooting Nerf hoops and slamming an energy drink, and agreed with Roger that the teachers should have spoken about this "poll thing" with him prior to meeting.

"These poll stunts are a pain, dude," Joel agreed.

"I've got to ask you though, Roger . . . how's it working for you, letting anyone in the building offer up things for your staff meeting agendas? Think about this . . . You have Sweet Polly Purebred on one side of the faculty meeting and Eddie Haskell on the other. Dude . . . you gonna trust them equally?!?

He continued, "Take for instance, when I involve a committee in making decisions . . . Like I tell my coaches . . . you *advise* . . . then *I* make the final decisions, myself. Period."

"What I do, Rog, is define the boundaries of conversation and, if I don't like 'em, I redefine 'em to my advantage. It gets a bit political at times, but hey . . . this is a political game we're in!! I certainly don't let teachers re-ink the boundaries on ANYTHING. That just doesn't work."

Roger said, "I guess that makes sense. I admit, Joel, I'm getting a bit worried, in that my next report to the superintendent is due quite soon. I think the school board is going to have their way with him if he can't serve up something new and nifty on improved learning real quick."

"Roger, dude . . . don't you see that if you lie belly-up on this parapro issue, the staff will have a list of others they wanted changed??

"I'm hoping, Joel, that if I cover this particular duty with paraprofessionals, I may be able to ask the teachers to give on other issues."

"Yeah . . . when I'm wearing a Speedo snowmobiling and whistling Dixie, that'll happen! Hey . . . I don't mean to be negative. Maybe you can make it work; you're a more popular guy than I am. Good luck to you, dude! Remember, Rog . . . BOUNDARIES. Gotta run!"

Roger thanked Joel Gerrymander for listening. He knew before he called Joel what he was going to do, and he was hoping that Joel would affirm his decision. From the tone of the conversation, Roger knew that Joel, in fact, did not support caving in to the staff, but rationalized that Joel had no idea how tough the situation he was in and how difficult it was telling this staff "No."

BELLY-UP

Roger e-mailed the staff later in the week that he would be able to use paraprofessionals to cover the before-school duty. He was a same-day rock star, receiving some nice e-mails, a couple of high fives, and even a plate of cookies.

That will go great with my popcorn this evening, Roger thought. *Some days, it is really great being the principal.*

Over popcorn and soda pop that evening, Roger's thoughts wandered as he continued thinking about the secret to a better path to a school-wide focus on learning.

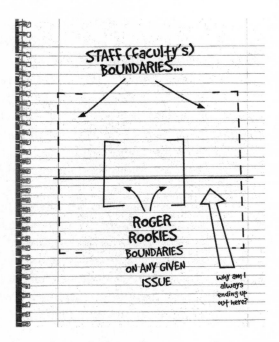

The following week, Karl Chameleon stopped into Roger's office.

"Hey, Mr. Rookie . . . do you have time to meet?"

"Always, Karl."

Roger asked Karl how everything was going and complimented him on his classroom. Karl exchanged pleasantries and got right down to business.

"Mr. Rookie, the math department is going to begin its graphing unit next month. We were hoping you would be able to support the math department by purchasing new graphing calculators."

Karl was quick to mention that they would not order a calculator for each student; instead, they would save money by only ordering classroom sets.

"How much is the price tag, Karl?" Roger asked.

Karl Chameleon smiled and produced three separate quotes that he had already worked on. The cheapest quote for the required number of calculators was $2,343. Roger thanked Karl for stopping in and doing the legwork on getting quotes for the calculators.

"What I'll do, Karl, is consider this request and get back with you and the department very soon."

When Karl Chameleon heard those words, he knew he was in trouble.

POINTING THE FINGER AT OTHERS

The next morning, Roger Rookie stopped in Karl Chameleon's room before school.

"Karl, I very much understand your need for calculators, but this one's a bit out of my hands, I admit. You know the crew from Central Office that I have to answer to. They're not going to budge and spend even one nickel more than what they budgeted for AMS."

He added, "If it were my decision, Karl, we would get you those calculators. I know what a great teacher you are, and this is a reasonable request. However, Central Office is forcing me to make budget reductions, and purchasing the calculators can't happen with those marching orders. I'm very sorry that this is our reality this year."

Karl Chameleon was disappointed, but thanked Roger Rookie for meeting with him and telling him face-to-face. He then ran to the teachers' lounge to share the news of how Central Office did not support the hard working staff at AMS.

This would not be the last time Roger blamed others for decisions.

UNINTENTIONAL CONSEQUENCES

Nellie Newcomer was flustered as she entered Sandy Starr's room.

"Hi, Nellie," said Sandy.

"Hi, Sandy. Do you have any ideas on how I can keep up with my struggling students when I'm no longer assigned to them in the morning? Now that they're all in the cafeteria, rather than in our classrooms, I'm not able to help them as well when I see they're falling behind."

"It frustrates me as well, Nellie. Have you thought about asking them down?"

"Yes, I've already done that, but they don't want to come. Evidently, they are allowed to sleep after arriving, which I don't believe is what was intended."

"Not intended, Nellie . . . but 'predicted,' I'm sad to say."

BOUNDARIES AND BULLETS

Roger read an article from his Principals Association newsletter that talked about boosting morale through site-based management. He thought, *What a great way to move forward with a positive climate! I'll form a site-based decision-making committee. Staff will love it!*

Roger had served on a building advisory committee as a teacher and really enjoyed having a voice in school decision making. At that time, he had several ideas that he thought would help more students experience success, and he believed in shared leadership. Maybe he could work with his staff and implement some at Anywhere Middle School.

He e-mailed the staff, asking for teacher volunteers to serve on the site-based decision making committee. Roger was excited, yet a bit shocked, when by the end of the day, he already had eight teachers indicate their interest in serving on the committee.

Bonus! He thought.

Then, Roger saw the list of names—not who Roger would have thought would volunteer extra time. In fact, three of The Bullies, Mildred Morose, Judy Slacker, and Edgar Sleeper, asked to be on the committee. Roger also noticed that none of his most effective teachers signed up for the committee.

Gosh . . . I was really hoping for Sandy Starr; even Karl Chameleon would be better than these folks, he grimaced.

Roger Rookie scheduled the first committee meeting. His main agenda item was increasing the communication between teachers and parents. Although he and a few other teachers contacted parents on a regular basis, the majority of AMS staff did not contact parents until there was a problem. Roger wanted a more proactive approach and believed the first contact from school should be on a positive note, no matter the student . . . no matter the parent.

"What do you mean, contact the parent when there's not a problem?" asked Mildred Morose. "The idea will not work. Positive support efforts have been tried and have not worked either. Plus, Roger, as we're sure you would agree, teachers are already overworked and underpaid."

Judy Slacker blurted out, "Until we change our students' parents, it does not matter what we do; some kids are just not going to get it."

Roger looked around the room in disbelief.

Mildred Morose then said, "I think I do have an option for us to consider that would make inroads to positive direction on this. Why don't we vote to give teachers additional planning time?"

Roger wanted to dodge this whole notion of voting on anything, as that was never his intention with the committee.

How is this going in a positive direction? He wondered. He needed to react quickly.

"Mrs. Morose, will you work with others on this committee and provide me with a detailed proposal?"

She smiled, the rest of the committee nodded, and Mildred Morose said, "We'll get right to work on this, Mr. Rookie."

Dodged that bullet, Roger said to himself.

The rest of the meeting was spent discussing concerns teachers had about students or procedures. Roger's committee idea felt more like a complaint department listening to folks who were unhappy with their jobs (and lives) than it did one of school improvement.

Roger Rookie left the meeting discouraged and wondered why he ever formed a site-based decision making committee. His only consolation was that Christmas break was in a few days and he would have a two-week break.

LAST DAY BEFORE BREAK

Anywhere Middle School always dismissed children right after lunch on the last day before a holiday break. As staff gathered for their afternoon holiday party, Roger Rookie thought of the large amount of money he had spent for gifts that he wrapped for a game in which faculty drew names and selected presents from a table; those who drew later in the game were able to steal from those who had drawn before.

Anywhere's paraprofessionals arrived a bit later than the rest of the staff and were all sitting together in a group, not appearing to have much of a good time. *Holidays aren't happy for everyone*, Roger thought to himself sadly. *Maybe this game will pick up their spirits.*

Teachers seem to be enjoying it for the most part, Roger mused, yet his mind wandered . . .

It's probably bad to think about this, but it feels as though I'm giving, giving, and giving . . . and those who don't give too awful much are tak-

*ing, taking, and taking. The more presents I dole out, the more it seems
that I'm expected to be Santa Claus. I love the positive atmosphere, as
the climate around here is most certainly better off than when I came.
But I'm wondering when we'll start turning the corner on some of these
things that will truly improve learning at our school.*

I'm wondering if what I'm doing is the secret solution after all.

"Merry Christmas, everyone, and a Happy New Year," Roger said as the
gifts were opened.

"Come on . . . a stupid candle?" Mildred Morose whispered.

"Cool . . . a coffee mug, for my deer blind," Karl Chameleon said.

"Merry Christmas, Nellie . . . we're so glad you're with us," said Sandy
Starr.

"Yeah . . . to take some of the load off the rest of us," chimed Judy
Slacker.

Roger concluded the gathering by saying, "Enjoy your time with family, and I look forward to your return after your most-deserved time with
loved ones and the holidays."

As he munched on holiday-flavored popcorn and drank eggnog-
flavored soda pop that evening, Roger's thoughts again went toward
finding the secret pathway to a school-wide focus on learning.

Roger returned from the two-week Christmas break ready to go, working even harder to win over the staff. The time away recharged his batteries, and he was fired up to keep the positive momentum at AMS moving. Roger continued to be visible in classrooms and kept writing notes to students, staff, and parents. He had noticed a few other teachers writing personal notes to students and parents.

School had been back in session a few days when Roger headed into school early to get some work done before staff and students arrived. Roger was halfway through his first cup of coffee when Mildred Morose walked in. His rejuvenated spirit quickly left his body, yet he tried not to let it show.

"Hello, Mrs. Morose, so very nice to see you . . . and so early in the morning."

Mildred decided to go with her fake nice voice; Roger played along.

After exchanging fake interest in each other's holiday breaks, Mildred stated, "Mr. Rookie, don't you think it is time to discuss my proposal . . . Uhh, I mean, the leadership team's proposal for additional planning time so departments could review data and plan interdisciplinary units?"

Roger did not believe for a minute that Mildred Morose was concerned with planning time or data; this was just another ploy of Mildred's to spend less time with students. Yet instead of being honest with Mildred and telling her that he thought time was better spent instructing students, Roger said the following:

"Mrs. Morose, your timing is well placed on this cordial visit, but I regret to inform you that the 'higher-ups' have denied this request."

Mildred shook her head, making several negative comments about the Central Office staff. "I have half a mind to get a petition started to throw the bum-of-a-superintendent out of his office," she snarled. "Please understand I say this in no way representing the views of the committee and, of course, with no disrespect to you, sir," she feigned.

Roger listened to her noxious comments; he felt guilty and disloyal for creating the problem. He hoped that the whole notion of a petition was just posturing and venom. He worried deep down about being "found out."

CHECKING ON THE NEWBIE

Roger scheduled another meeting with Nellie Newcomer. He had noticed during walk-throughs that, although her lessons were creative and students appeared engaged, Nellie seemed not quite her usual perky self. When Roger entered her room, he could not help but be impressed with how organized she was. Nellie Newcomer utilized her limited square footage as well as the most veteran teacher in the district. He sat in a student desk next to Nellie's.

"How are things going for you, Nellie?" he asked.

"Christmas break helped recharge my batteries, Mr. Rookie, and I believe that I am ready for the second semester. Please offer me any advice that you can provide, as I would very much appreciate it."

Nellie had learned a lot her first semester about working with students and the challenges of trying to help every student be successful. She was a very popular teacher, although some students took advantage of her kindness from time to time. As she was a newbie, they were able to pull the wool over her eyes here and there, but she was a quick learner.

Roger asked, "What's been your relationship with other staff members, Nellie? Are you finding that 'fit' and professional family that we all desire?"

Nellie responded, "Mrs. Starr and a small group of teachers have really been helpful in helping me learn the routines and strategies to help struggling learners."

Roger agreed with Nellie and said that Sandy was a great role model for all educators. "How about Mrs. Slacker?" he inquired.

Nellie looked at Roger and said in a matter-of-fact manner, "Mrs. Slacker has not met with me since long before Christmas; we really don't have a relationship. Whenever I need help, I ask other teachers whom I've gotten to know and trust."

Nellie had met a nice group of teachers when they stopped by her room the first couple of weeks, and they had each sent her notes and e-mails throughout the first semester offering their help and encouragement.

Nellie then looked at Roger and said in a very quiet voice, "Mr. Rookie, please forgive me for saying this, but Mrs. Slacker should never again be allowed to be a mentor. She has never appeared to care about me, and from what I've witnessed so far, she is not somebody I would ever want to use as a role model."

Roger Rookie had a big lump in his throat. He told Nellie, "I'm very sorry you have not had a good experience with Mrs. Slacker."

As Roger walked out of the room, he grimaced at the thought of allowing Judy Slacker to be a mentor. He thought to himself, *Nellie was a first-year teacher who needed support and deserved better. I have nobody to blame but myself, especially since I didn't even speak with Judy about her responsibilities as a mentor like I told Nellie I would. I'm sitting here searching for the secret to better student learning, and it seems at times that I'm keeping a secret from myself . . . that glad-handing and over-adapting to others may not be making our problems go away or get better. I feel like such a heel.* Despite these apprehensions, Roger did feel, on balance, that the school had turned the corner with regard to climate. He was hoping that a new way of doing business—getting along with each other—was making at least a small difference.

It IS tiring, though. Some nights, I just can't believe how quickly I crash when I get home, Roger admitted to himself.

On the bright side, students, teachers, staff members, and parents appeared to be happy with AMS. The school had a more positive environment. However, Roger knew the building was still falling short regarding its test scores. The school's student achievement data showed that many students were not performing at grade level, and AMS data were lower than most of the schools in the entire district.

At the end of the day, I just know I'm going to be on the hook for these test scores, thought Roger. *It seems like I'm climbing the steps to success as fast as I can . . . and even bringing lots of folks with me. They're happy; they LIKE me. I'm in their classes, making lots of positive calls home on the teachers' behalf, and I'm even welcome in the lounge at times. The problem is, I wonder if I'm on the right stairway.*

MID-YEAR EVALUATION

Roger waited anxiously for a meeting with his superintendent. It was his mid-year evaluation, and he was very nervous. A report on AMS's focus on school-wide learning was to be part of the discussion, as was his plan for the upcoming month of high-stakes tests.

Those are the test scores that Carol Charming never forgets about, he worried.

Fidgeting with his folder and pen, and doodling feverishly, he could not help but garner the attention of Cindy Sage, the superintendent's secretary, who sat outside his office.

Cindy had been serving superintendents in Anywhere for over thirty years. She was a local girl, born and raised here, and married to a traveling executive who showed few signs of slowing down in his own career. Cindy Sage was on her fifth superintendent and planned retirement a few years hence, once her last child was out of college. She was a quiet, meticulous, loyal administrative professional, with deep knowledge of the district and an understanding of the laundry of all who had worked in it for over three decades.

She very much liked Roger Rookie, as she thought of him as another son. She had four.

"Roger, the superintendent is taking calls regarding last night's board meeting; it looks like it will be another fifteen to twenty minutes. Can I get you a cup of coffee?"

"No, thank you, ma'am. I appreciate it, though."

She looked, as he appeared to doodle more nervously in his scratch pad.

"Roger, why don't you come over here for a few, and sit down in the lounge area with me. I have a few minutes, and I would like to talk. Would you mind?"

"Well, I guess not. That would be nice. Every time I stop, it seems we're always so busy."

She said inquisitively, "Please tell me how things are going, Roger. I once was a student at Anywhere. I have known every teacher and principal in that building for the last thirty years, and I have been quite interested in how you would do in the post-Neverthere era." She chuckled.

"Ned Neverthere, that old fella. Did you know he and I graduated together from high school, Roger?"

"No, ma'am. But it's a small world, isn't it?"

"It sure is, Roger. You know, between you and me, I figured it was going to be a bit rough on you at first. You seem to be handling yourself well."

"Why's that, Mrs. Sage?"

"Ned Neverthere didn't exactly leave you with a well-oiled machine in AMS. What once was the shiniest star in the district—Ned's leadership, that is—lost a bit of its luster near the end. Now I adore Ned, so I'll say no more, but the focus on learning did slip away from him, and it seems as though it is a pretty tough nut to crack at this point."

"Glad to hear that someone realizes it, ma'am. I'm trying hard to turn things around, yet I'm thinking now that it may take a bit more time than my boss is going to allow."

"Does that have you worried, Roger?"

"Yeah . . . a bit. But I'm an optimist. I'm working on figuring out the secret to this whole thing, and I hope that I'm on the right path."

"Would you like to share? With thirty years in this office, having put four boys and a girl through the school system, and watching my share of principals wield their leadership with hundreds of staff and thousands of students . . . I might be able to give you a good, honest perspective. I'll probably learn a bit from what you've done, too."

"Thanks for asking," said Roger. "Do we have about ten minutes or so?"

"I'll bet we have another fifteen or twenty," said Cindy Sage.

"Here goes."

Roger shared with Cindy Sage what was happening at Anywhere Middle School. She listened intently as he shared his struggles getting the staff to embrace the changes that he felt would be beneficial for students. Cindy did not ask a lot of questions, yet listened actively. Roger avoided mentioning some of the changes he had made to appease the teachers, but Cindy had seen too many new principals not to know the dynamics of what probably went on. To Roger's surprise, once he finally shared with Cindy all the stuff that had been happening in an effort to change to a focus on learning, rather than on teaching, he actually felt good about getting it off his shoulders.

"Roger, I want you to know that your confidence placed in me is admirable."

Cindy Sage sat quietly and processed Roger's comments. One of her best qualities was that she did not judge people and had a great way of asking questions that could lead a person to finding his or her own solution. Her first question was, "Roger, if you could wave a magic wand, what would your perfect school look like?"

Roger wasted no time. "I want a school that, when you walk in, you know it is a place you want your son or daughter to attend. I want a school where staff members collaborate and work as a team and where the focus of meetings and professional development is on how the school could improve so that every student learns and develops to his or her potential."

"What do you believe, Roger, is preventing AMS from being that school?"

"Teachers, it seems; especially the building leadership team, who continue to raise issues with every idea that requires teachers to teach differently," he responded. "It seems as if AMS is more about meeting the needs of teachers than it is about students. Now don't get me wrong, Mrs. Sage, I am working on this, and I think I'm figuring out the secret. But it's taking just a bit more time than I was thinking it would at first."

"Sounds challenging, indeed, Roger."

"I have made some huge moves toward better relationships, which are positioning us to head in the right direction and which I'm hoping the boss will concur have been beneficial."

Roger feigned optimism, in actuality.

He trusted Cindy Sage, but at the same time realized that she was his boss's confidential secretary, so it wasn't his nature to let too much out of the bag. He thought of The Bullies and their leader, Mildred Morose, and how he would get nervous before faculty meetings because of this group. He thought also of Mildred's rude behavior. He thought of all the time he spent each day solving management problems in an attempt to keep staff happy. He thought about how much time this was taking away from moving the building forward academically.

Roger then thought of his secretary, Trudy Savage—her behavior, and the negative impact it had upon AMS. He thought about his numerous attempts at trying to change Trudy Savage's behavior by killing her with kindness and hoping his positive attitude would rub off on her.

He thought that, although the building climate was 100 percent better than when he arrived and several teachers had shared that with him, in other areas the school was a long way from what he had hoped for. He thought about . . . .

"Roger . . . Roger . . . are you still with me?" asked Cindy Sage, with a warm smile.

"Yes, ma'am," Roger said with a bit of sweat on his brow, realizing that he had been lost in thought. Thoughts he wasn't prepared to share.

"You must have a lot on your mind, Roger. That's natural for one assuming so much leadership at such a young age in one's career."

Cindy Sage then asked, "How many teacher evaluations have you done, Roger?"

Roger thought for a moment and said, "Mrs. Sage, I have completed about six, with another six to do on this year's rotation."

"It might not be my business to pry, Roger, but were any of the evaluations with teachers that are NOT helping you create the ideal school you described earlier?"

Roger felt himself tense up, knowing the answer was yes. He was embarrassed to admit that he had been overly positive in his evaluations and had not given the teachers constructive feedback and actions to improve instruction at AMS.

"How are your new teachers doing? And . . . more importantly, Roger . . . are they eating lunch with the right people?"

To this, Roger answered, "Very well, thank you . . . and yes, Nellie Newcomer, for one, is spending much time with Sandy Starr." Roger did not mention who he assigned as her mentor.

"That's excellent news," said Mrs. Sage, yet closely watching Roger who appeared deep in thought again. *What an idiot I have been allowing the most veteran, yet negative, teachers to serve as mentors instead of assuring that our best teachers match up well with new hires,* he pondered.

Cindy Sage let Roger's thoughts hang in the air for awhile and then said, "Roger, you know best what the REAL strengths, weaknesses, and opportunities are at Anywhere Middle School. It is not going to take your superintendent or your mid-year evaluation to sort these out. I think you have done a bit of this today while sitting here with me."

"And for what it is worth, I believe you have within you the ability and the smarts to take Anywhere Middle School from where it is now to that 'better place' you described to me just a few minutes ago."

"Thank you, Mrs. Sage. It means a lot that you have such confidence in me. I'm not going to let anyone down. We'll move this place forward, that's for sure."

Roger then focused as he heard the telephone call wrapping up in the other room. *I have an opinion as to what the problem is at AMS,* he thought. *The problem with Anywhere Middle School is that the students and staff need a strong leader, somebody willing to get the right stakeholders working toward a shared vision. The staff needs a leader who knows his core values and focuses on the needs of students. A leader can never blame the higher-ups for something he's gutless about doing. My actions of late have suggested that I am more interested in making friends than being a true leader. That's no way to improve learning. That's simply a way to share smiles, and still end up getting stabbed in the back. I have been keeping a secret from myself—the fact that a leader needs to hold others accountable, as well as himself.*

Roger would never forget the words that Cindy Sage spoke, as well as her calm reassurance and confidence in him. He needed to grow up, put on his big boy pants, and find the secret that had been eluding him. In his determination not to act like Ned Neverthere, he had become a cheerleader instead, trying to be everyone's friend at the expense of helping children succeed. The teachers liked Roger Rookie, but Roger was pretty confident that most of the staff did not respect him.

Roger took the weekend to reflect on his actions the past few months. He was so focused on trying to get people to like him that he lost focus of why he had become an administrator—to make a difference for students and staff. Roger had to rethink his leadership style in finding the secret solution, his pathway to leadership success.

TEACHERS' LOUNGE

"Hey Babble, we hear Rookie is coming in to do your evaluation next week," said Mildred Morose. "What sort of a dog and pony show do you have planned for the boy?"

"Nothing much, Mildred. Like you think ANY of us are going to get a bad evaluation?? We were here long before Rookie took off his training wheels, and we'll be here long after he leaves, which by my estimation is roughly 110 days away."

Laughter.

"Hey, did you hear how many principals it takes to form a building leadership committee?" asked Karl.

"Oh, come on, Chameleon . . . don't quit your day job!"

"Three—one to write up an agenda that we'll choose to ignore . . . another to take two weeks to make the decision Mildred wants anyway . . . and a third to miss the fact that by the time we negotiate our next contract, we'll all be getting paid a stipend to spend our time SERVING on that site-based decision making committee!"

Laughter.

"Hey . . . any luck with your calculators, you doorknob!"

"C'mon, guys . . . give me time. I'll be golfing with someone from Central Office at the Athletic League Scramble, and I'll find out who's telling Rookie 'No.'"

"Where's Judy Slacker today?"

"She left early again. Something about a very important meeting at the department store."

Laughter.

"Hey . . . staff meeting tomorrow a.m. Rise and shine early, my fellow fools! Lounge bet—How many think that our resident goody-two-shoes combo, Sandy and our new 'Sandy, Jr.,' will sit again in the front row, sucking up as usual?"

"Darn well better have a bit more variety on the menu," said Mildred Morose. "Otherwise, we'll have to give Rookie a bit of a tune-up as to the lifestyle we are accustomed to living around here."

Laughter.

THE COFFEE KLATCH

"I feel so much better about my mid-year evaluation, Mrs. Starr," said Nellie Newcomer. "Mr. Rookie gave me quite high marks for planning, instructional delivery, and assessment, yet I still have a ways to go in classroom control."

"Sounds like you are doing as well as anyone would expect," Sandy Starr responded.

"The only thing I'm a bit confused about," said Nellie, "is exactly HOW I am to improve my classroom control. Mr. Rookie says not to let students take advantage of me or 'pull my chain,' as he calls it, but when I ask him for specifics, he says it's all about finding these secrets over time. Are the techniques for success really supposed to be discovered? If so, can you at least give me a hint?"

Sandy Starr responded, "We're all so busy, Nellie. Mr. Rookie included. Why don't you and I spend a bit of time after school tomorrow talking through some of these situations, as it appears that we'll need to find another way of providing you this good advice that you need this time of year. I'll help you out, but let us keep this between you and me. With Judy as your mentor . . . well, allegedly anyway . . . we wouldn't want to raise the ire of her group, now would we?"

Sandy Starr thought to herself, *Maybe if Roger Rookie would spend a little less time placating those who care much less for children and much more for stipends, we would have a more effective induction and mentoring process around Anywhere Middle School. If I weren't so busy with standardized tests approaching, I would ask for a meeting with him myself, as I am a bit concerned that he is being led around by the people who are not going to move our children's performance forward.*

"Can I ask you another thing, Mrs. Starr?"

"Certainly, Nellie."

"Has Karl Chameleon been acting a bit different lately?"

"Why do you ask?"

"Well, when I first took this job, he was always in his class next door with students having a good time. We would spend time between classes talking, and he even taught me a number of students' names. Over the past few months, I haven't seen him as often, as he is spending much more time in the lounge."

"Nothing good is going to come out of that," Sandy Starr responded.

"I hear him yelling at students a bit more, which wasn't at all like him the first part of this year. I'm just worried about him, that's all."

"Nellie, you have reason to be. He's not in good company."

ROGER ROOKIE'S DEEP THOUGHTS

THE GLAD-HANDER'S EFFECTS ON STAFF...

SUPERSTARS
- Like it at first
- Get frustrated with unsolved problems
- Do NOT feel valued because all are treated the same

FENCESITTERS
- Love it!
- Do little work but feel entitled
- Their efforts go up at 1st, then diminish

BULLIES
- Continually become more demanding
- Milk the Leader
- Have an underserved confidence level

THE GLAD-HANDER
CONTINUED...

THE LEADER FEELS
- Good for a very brief period
- That what he/she does is NEVER enough
- Taken advantage of

UNINTENDED CONSEQUENCES
- organization becomes unfocused
- over time, less work gets done
- The Leader gains, then loses RESPECT

4

ROGER ROOKIE'S THIRD MAKEOVER: THE THUMB

When Roger was a student teacher at Blue Collar Middle School, his principal was Ivan Ironside. Ironside, a former military captain with shaved head that kept widening to the shoulders, was a no-nonsense principal.

As a student teacher, Roger marveled at the tight ship he ran. Ironside was actually a bit intimidating. As Roger recalled, he had complete control over every situation. Many of the problems that Roger was experiencing as a principal weren't present in Ironside's school. Roger gave Ironside all the credit. He couldn't imagine a teacher mouthing off to Ivan Ironside. Certainly no one would dare stab him in the back . . . . he might turn around and clean their clock!

I need to talk with Mr. Ironside and get his advice on how to turn things around at Anywhere Middle School, Roger thought. So he called Ironside's secretary, who set up a meeting. *It will be nice to see things at Blue Collar again . . . it's been a while.*

As he parked his car at Blue Collar Middle School, he saw a custodian busily sweeping the front walk. Another was polishing the front handrails adjacent to the steps. A physical education class could be seen in the distance doing jumping jacks and push-ups.

Boy . . . it's cold weather, and these kids are outside! In my school, even the teachers would refuse to suit up for outside calisthenics.

As Roger Rookie walked to the front door, he saw a student hurry down from the office to open it, greeting him with a "Welcome, sir, to Blue Collar Middle School, where we do more before 9 a.m. than most do all day!"

"Thank you, young man. I'm here to meet with Mr. Ironside."

"He would be right up the stairs, sir . . . just past our dress code checkpoint, next to the teachers' lesson-plan submission window. Have a nice day."

Roger spent a few moments catching up with a few of the secretaries who remembered him as a student teacher. One gave him a hug, the other pinched his cheek. They couldn't believe that he was all grown up, and a principal at that!

Roger then sat quietly and awaited the appearance of Ivan Ironside. He noticed a few other teachers waiting for him. They would be ushered into his office quickly by the secretaries, stay for a few moments, then quickly walk back out again and down the hallways, serious in gait, many with heads down, . . . all tending to the business of "doing school."

What a machine! Roger marveled. *"In," quickly . . . "Out," expediently . . . and all with a "Yes, sir . . . and can I have another?" look on their faces. Now THIS is leadership!*

"ROOKIE! I hear you're a principal now, young man! Any truth to that rumor??"

Roger stood quickly, snapping to attention, arms at his side and feet together. In front of him, Ivan Ironside inspecting him from top to bottom, with the same martial pose he remembered.

"At ease, Rookie, you're one of us now. How've you been, young man?"

"Very busy, Mr. Ironside. Thank you for taking time with me today."

As they sat down for coffee, Roger's heart rate increased. Ironside, although not intending to, still intimidated him.

"Rookie . . . my secretary tells me you're here for advice. If you and I were on a social visit, we'd go out into the woods and spend time shooting things. Since that's not the case, there's no time to shoot anything, not even 'the bull.' Just give me the facts. The sooner I understand your theater of operation, the sooner we can deploy something."

"Yes, Mr. Ironside. It all began with . . ."

Roger told Ironside about the course of events that began the past summer, as well as the launch of the school year. He told him about teachers complaining about Seminar . . . about their before-school duty . . . about the dysfunctional faculty meetings . . . and all the money he had spent on food. . . .

"I have this group that I call . . ."

Before Roger could say, "The Bullies" (and it was probably fortunate that he did not), Ironside interrupted and said, "Stop! Rookie, who is running the show over there!?! You need to man-UP and start leading! I know you're still wet behind the ears, but, good grief, quit rolling belly-up for an abdominal scratch. People are walking all over you."

Ironside continued, "You've been in my school; do you think I got my staff in tip-top shape by kissing everybody's backside all day?"

Roger shook his head. He asked, "But how do you keep the morale of the staff up?"

Ironside replied, "You want to know how to have good morale?? Accomplish your mission! When I was a captain in the military, my soldiers had great morale when we implemented my plan, and it was successful. When they didn't do things the right way, I chewed their butts. Are you hearing me, kid? You think your staff respects you? Based on what I am hearing, the answer is a big fat NO. Stop acting like a patsy. Start leading!"

Mr. Ironside segued into stories of his early days in the service, where he honed and crafted his leadership under arduous conditions and how, once stateside, he "took command" of his teaching staff the way he worked with recruits overseas.

"You have to be direct with your people" he concluded. "They work for YOU, not the other way around. Tell them what you want from them; command respect, and above all . . . accomplish your mission. You're not there to make friends, and you're certainly not their darn bellhop. Stop pussyfooting around and put your thumb on those people!"

Roger thanked Ivan Ironside for meeting with him and giving him advice on how to fix the problems at AMS.

BACK AT ANYWHERE

Anywhere Middle School had a faculty meeting scheduled for the following week. Roger had a few days to prepare for the meeting. In doing so, he put one word on the faculty meeting agenda—CHANGE.

Roger Rookie kept reflecting on Ironside's advice, and that only fueled his fire. He installed a new mirror in his office, full length so that he could practice his new martial pose. He bought a few new suits, charcoal . . . darker than what he typically would wear, with power ties in red, white, and blue. Shiny, black patent leather shoes with squared toes were a bit uncomfortable for him, but he was trying to get used to them.

Roger Rookie even hung a few pictures of leaders he now chose to admire, most of whom won battles of one kind or another. He ordered a bigger chair for his desk. There were still three months left in the school year, and Roger Rookie was determined to use "real leadership" to improve Anywhere Middle School. The last thing he thought before he walked into the faculty meeting was, *MY way or the highway*!

He scribbled a few thoughts onto his notepad.

ADVICE FROM
MR. IRONSIDE

1. YOU ARE NOT A PATSY...
     START LEADING!

2. DON'T KISS PEOPLE'S (yuck...
     BACKSIDES!   went
                            visual
                            on that
                            one) :͜
3. BE DIRECT...
     RESULTS WILL WIN
     RESPECT!
     (I think "this" is THE SECRET)

The faculty meeting began promptly at 7:30.

"Welcome, ladies and gentlemen. Let's get right to the topic of changing this school, and make sure you take notes on what we'll be deploying. You'll have your marching orders shortly."

Teachers, a bit confused, looked around at each other and, in a few cases, thought Roger Rookie's new style was a bit cute as he tried it on for size.

"Did he spend the weekend watching General Patton movies? Whispered Edgar to Karl, pretending to slap him with a glove. Karl chuckled, but quickly stopped when Roger snapped a look in their direction.

LaVon Babble then walked in late, carrying a coffee and talking on her cell phone.

Roger Rookie looked directly at LaVon and said in a loud voice, "Mrs. Babble, you continue to arrive late for meetings and interrupt our work with your private conversation. It is rude and will not be tolerated. You need to leave."

LaVon Babble dropped her phone. The room was silent.

Roger Rookie pointed his finger at the door.

LaVon picked up her cell phone, looked at The Bullies, who simply looked back at her, and then walked out of the room. Roger then turned to the staff with a click of his heel, prepared if anybody wanted to challenge his authority.

Mildred Morose stood up and began to speak. "Mr. Rookie, on behalf of the staff who just witnessed your handling of Mrs. Babble's arrival. . . ."

Roger interrupted, "Mrs. Morose, you can sit down and be quiet or join Mrs. Babble, your choice."

Roger's inside voice was incongruous with his outside demeanor.

What the heck are you doing, Roger, it said. *You're really out there on a limb, and you're liable to get it chopped off!* He was sure that he might have a heart attack any minute, but continued to glare at Mrs. Morose.

Mildred mumbled something that the other Bullies heard, but sat back down.

Roger returned to his agenda. Using the new pointer stick he bought from a military surplus store over the weekend, he then paced back and forth in front of the portable screen set up for the meeting, tapping on the projected data from the standardized test scores the school had recently received.

He then stopped his march, turning "left face" to the staff, and said, "These data are terrible. What do you think Central Office is going to think of these data?"

Staff just looked at him with "deer in headlights" expressions.

"Well, guess what? Things are going to change around here."

"ALL staff will be held accountable for making AMS a premier school. It's going to start with doing your jobs! I don't want to hear if you DO or DON'T like this or that . . . 'Blah, blah, blah.'"

Roger marched back and forth, continuing, "If you don't like how prepared students are when they come to class, contact the parents yourselves! If you don't like some of the working conditions here at Anywhere, be thankful that you have a place to work! If you don't like getting to meetings on time and paying attention, then find someplace to work where you can show up late and read the newspaper! Most of all, remember that I'm your principal, not your concierge."

Roger spent the last ten minutes outlining what those changes entailed with respect to their curriculum, instruction, and student supervision. The meeting ended promptly at 8:00. Roger did not see any teachers checking papers, texting, or talking like he routinely saw during staff meetings.

He felt empowered.

It dawned on Roger as staff filed out of the room that not a single teacher spoke during the last half hour of the meeting. Roger made a mental note to call Ivan Ironside and thank him for telling him how a leader behaves.

STUDENT ISSUES

The morning's docket was to be filled with Roger dealing with student discipline. Coming off the faculty meeting victory, he decided to continue with his new leadership style. Several students had been sent to the office from the same classrooms that always sent students to the office. Roger Rookie was sick of seeing the same students.

He decided it was time to treat students like he had just treated the staff. Roger called the first student into his office. "Why were you sent down here?" he asked.

"Well, Mr. Rookie, I simply left my homework in my locker, and I was kicked out for no reason."

"Last time I thought about a student's job description," said Roger, "it involved using the five minutes between classes to go to your locker, grab your materials for the next class, and then proceed to that destination prepared for instruction. Am I correct!?!"

"But Mr. Rookie ..."

"NO BUTs!! Talking to you about leaving your homework in your locker is a waste of your parents' and taxpayers' money! You should be in class doing *student* things, and I should be in my office doing *principal* things!! Talking about a part of your job description that a kindergartner could understand is embarrassing for both YOU and ME. Have some pride. Get your act together!"

The student sat quietly until Mr. Rookie was done speaking.

"I'm giving you three nights of detention to teach you a lesson about your job description as a student. Off you go!!"

When Roger opened his office door, the other students waiting to see him looked at him with big eyes.

Roger met with the next student. However, unlike the first student, when Roger raised his voice, the student argued right back. As the conversation escalated and inappropriate comments were made, Roger suspended the student.

In fact, he suspended a boatload of students that day. And a boatload the next.

Roger decided he'd had enough of students getting sent to the office for stupid reasons. He sent the following e-mail to the staff:

Faculty,

Over the past few months, I have noticed an increasing number of frivolous student referrals to my office, which have resulted in a loss of instructional time and decreased productivity for the office. Effective immediately, silly issues like forgotten pencils and homework left in lockers will be the responsibility of the teachers to correct. If students are sent to the office, it had better be for a good reason that is beyond the control of a professional faculty member to handle. In short, if you send a student to me, it will be an admission that you are unable to handle the situation, which may result in a meeting afterward for further training and corrective action on your behalf. If you have any problems with this new protocol, see me.

Educationally yours,

Mr. Rookie

ON PATROL

Roger was walking through the school when he noticed that Edgar Sleeper was not fulfilling his corridor supervision responsibility. Teachers were required to supervise the hallways between classes to keep students moving along and curtail inappropriate behavior. Roger walked into Edgar's room and saw him sitting at his desk talking on his cell phone.

"Mr. Sleeper, why are you not on duty?"

Edgar quickly ended the phone call, saying, "Sorry, Mr. Rookie, important telephone call that needed my attention. I'll get right out in the hall."

"Electronic technology does not have a constitutional right to be answered during your professional working hours, Mr. Sleeper. Was there a death in the family?"

"No, Mr. Rookie . . . but . . ."

"Did someone lose a limb through amputation?"

"No . . . but . . ."

"Did you win the lottery, and thus will no longer have a need for employment at Anywhere?"

"No . . . but . . ."

"Then, in my estimation, it was still your responsibility to supervise the hallway, and you were clearly not fulfilling your duty. You can expect a letter in your file noting the indiscretion."

Roger turned quickly, "about face," walked down to his office, and sent out another school-wide e-mail:

Faculty,

While on rounds today, I noticed that staff were not fulfilling their professional corridor supervision responsibilities, as outlined in the performance expectations checklist provided to you at the outset of this school year. Faculty and staff found derelict of duty in the aforementioned will be handled according to the progressive and corrective disciplinary measures found in this year's Anywhere Middle School Staff Handbook. I thank you for your anticipated cooperation.

Responsibly yours,

Mr. Rookie

Trudy Savage then appeared proudly at his door with a stack of Post-It notes . . . on them, names and telephone numbers of angry parents. Lots of names; lots of notes.

"It's about time someone started making up for lost time, whipping these little heathens into shape," she said, scattering the notes across Roger's desk. "I took the liberty of telling these deadbeats, sir, that you'll call back when you're darned good and ready, and that they'll rue the day they complained to Roger Rookie!"

"This looks like I'll be making calls long into the evening," said Roger.

"Nah . . . just tell them the way it's gonna be, and hang up. Not rocket science!!"

Trudy Savage added, "I'll leave the door ajar; don't worry about keeping your voice down, it will help with deterrence."

She spun around, left his office, and barked at someone in the distance.

Roger got home very late that evening and devoured some late-night television, popcorn, and his favorite soda. He reflected on his newfound Ironside style.

He had to admit, certain parts of this new, tough attitude made the day go very well. The faculty meeting went well, and he was certain that office referrals would decrease. Yet there were other parts of the day he did not feel as good about. Yelling at students was not at all a fit for him; neither was arguing to the point that they used profanity and got themselves suspended. Roger decided he just needed to give the new style more time and that people would adjust their behavior and actions once they got used to the new sheriff in town, Roger Rookie, and that the law ain't for sale at Anywhere no more!

Later in the week, Roger Rookie e-mailed LaVon Babble about meeting in his office.

> Mrs. Babble,
>   Plan on arriving in my office within five minutes of tomorrow's closing bell to discuss the incident of your tardiness at our most recent staff meeting. Your tardiness at this meeting, if it occurs, will not reflect favorably on the outcome.
>   Promptly yours,
>   Mr. Rookie

LaVon Babble usually left school early to pick up her children, but she could sense that she had better make other arrangements for her children and attend the meeting. After LaVon's short wait in the outer office, where she felt like a student waiting to be disciplined, Roger Rookie finally opened his door and signaled for her to come in.

Roger Rookie looked directly at LaVon Babble and said, "Mrs. Babble, as your principal, I am directing you from this date forward to be on time and attentive for future faculty meetings. Further, texting, checking papers, or talking while presentations are being made will be grounds for your removal from the meetings."

He then shared with LaVon Babble what was discussed at the staff meeting.

Roger closed the meeting by saying, "Mrs. Babble, you no longer have permission to leave early at the end of the day. If you cannot fulfill your contract, although my desk is full, I will find room on it for you to place your letter of resignation."

Roger Rookie then stood up and walked out of the office.

After a few minutes, LaVon Babble got up and left as well. Trudy Savage couldn't help but notice the tears on her face as she exited Roger Rookie's office. Looking back over her shoulders, she made a quiet phone call to the teachers' lounge.

The Smith parent meeting was held in Roger Rookie's office. Roger began the meeting with introductions, and then asked the parents to state their concerns.

"Mr. Rookie, our seventh grade daughter's grades are not at all acceptable; they have gone down each quarter. We would like to request help to get our daughter back on the right track."

"Mr. and Mrs. Smith, have teachers been in contact with you to keep you updated on your daughter's performance?"

"Some of the teachers had been in contact with us," said Mrs. Smith, "But we have not heard at all from two teachers despite our continued attempts to share our e-mail address, our work telephone numbers, and available times for meetings."

Roger immediately asked Trudy Savage to call the two teachers down to join them in the meeting.

He then stated, with the teachers present, that this neglect of duty was unacceptable and he apologized to the parents for their lack of follow-up. He shared that he would follow up privately with the teachers and that the Smith family could expect frequent updates in the future. Both teachers did not say a word and kept their heads down. The meeting concluded with the guidance counselor arranging for the parents and teachers to use a notebook journal for daily feedback and communication.

"Off you go!" said Roger Rookie to the two teachers. He then showed the Smiths to the school entrance and thanked them for their visit.

Roger Rookie was to observe Karl Chameleon's class. Karl was talking with students as Roger entered the room. However, as Karl began his lesson, he couldn't help thinking about how much Roger had changed in recent weeks and how rudely he was treating teachers. The teachers' lounge had become a therapy room for teachers who had been bullied by "Robo-Rookie" as many now called Roger behind his back.

Staff also noticed that Roger was sporting a new haircut that made him look like he had enlisted in the Marines. Karl Chameleon stumbled his way through the lesson and was not at his best with Roger in the room. He dreaded his post-observation conference, afraid of the criticism and potential attack. For the first time in a long time, Karl Chameleon thought about applying for a job at another school.

Nellie Newcomer arrived for a meeting in Roger Rookie's office. Roger had been so busy telling people what to do, he had not had the chance to meet with Nellie in several weeks. Nellie stopped at the entry to Roger's office and waited for him to give her permission to enter his office.

"Come in, please, Miss Newcomer," Roger said.

After Nellie sat down, Roger began by saying, "Miss Newcomer, I continue to be impressed by your skills. Your lessons are creative, and students are always engaged when I observe your classroom. Further, you have one of the most organized classrooms at AMS and, in nearly one year, you have established yourself as a quality teacher. Given this, what would you like to discuss with me at this time?"

Nellie then brought up her mentor, Judy Slacker. "Mr. Rookie, nothing has changed since the last time we met. I can only count on one hand the number of times that Mrs. Slacker has met with me the entire year. I'm sorry to bring this up to you, but you have asked for my candor and I respect your authority."

Mr. Rookie thanked Nellie for meeting with him and, as she left for her classroom, he immediately turned around and began typing on his computer. Roger had eight months of pent-up frustration with Judy Slacker's horrible job of mentoring Nellie, and his frustration was coming out. In a note to her he demanded a meeting for the next day before school started.

Mrs. Slacker,

   It has come to my attention that you have continued to disregard my expectation that you provide mentoring to Miss Newcomer during her first year of teaching at Anywhere Middle School. I am thus directing you to a meeting in my office to be scheduled a half hour prior to the start of school tomorrow morning. I trust you will be on time.

   With concern and disappointment,
   Principal Rookie

Judy Slacker arrived for school, walked quickly down to Roger Rookie's office, and found him sitting at his desk. As she entered his office, Roger said, "Mrs. Slacker, will you please close the door."

Roger Rookie continued, "Mrs. Slacker, you have failed miserably in your duties as Miss Newcomer's mentor. You have disregarded my admonitions to you with willful and wanton callousness to the needs of someone new to our profession. I am now beyond dismay at your professional performance; I am ANGRY!"

Roger Rookie's shouting at Mrs. Slacker could be heard in the outer office. He demanded that she begin meeting WEEKLY with Nellie Newcomer. He warned Judy Slacker that he would be checking up, and if she did not obey his directions, there would be discipline for insubordination. She did not say a single word during the meeting.

ANOTHER MEETING, THUMB-STYLE

Roger Rookie was two months into his new style. Students and staff seemed to have adjusted to how Roger wanted things done. Unlike earlier in the year when students and teachers came to Roger all the time, now almost nobody spoke with him. Although Roger missed talking to students, he did not miss always solving the teachers' problems. Yes, Roger felt like things were finally coming around at Anywhere Middle School.

Roger reviewed the agenda for the next faculty meeting. He didn't bother buying any food as he used to do. He had a lot of stuff to get through, so he decided to skip Positive Comments. He quickly took roll, a new thing Roger had implemented to make sure all staff members were in attendance and on time.

With a smile, he said, "I'm pleased that there is again perfect attendance today. We have some very important areas of focus that I want to highlight, as we are nearing the end of our academic year. Now take note: before I discuss these in detail, even though there are only a few weeks of school left, AMS is NOT going to start playing games and watching movies. I expect during my walk-throughs that I will see teachers teaching and students learning."

"Are there any questions?"

None.

Roger continued, "I also need to see more teachers supervising un-structured areas, specifically the hallways between classes. As you know, I've already had to reprimand a few of you for dereliction of duty."

A few heads went down with this comment. He was pleased that Mildred Morose did not make eye contact, yet what Roger Rookie did not notice was that Sandy Starr and Nellie Newcomer didn't either.

From The Bullies, and even a few others, there were looks of contempt and passive aggressiveness, yet Roger did not pick up on these.

Roger asked again, "Are there any questions?"

None.

Roger finished the agenda, noting his areas of instructional focus, and teachers filed out.

THUMBLAND MURMERS

Roger arrived early to school to finish some paperwork before his morning patrol. As he made his rounds, he heard his name mentioned. Roger slowed down and eavesdropped on the conversation. He couldn't wait to crack on this group of malcontents that were most likely poisoning his school.

As Mr. Rookie continued to listen, however, he realized the voice was Sandy Starr's, one of his best teachers.

Mrs. Starr continued, "I am very uncomfortable with anybody in the building, students or staff members, being treated disrespectfully. Mr. Sleeper shared with me that he was talking on his cell phone with his mother who is battling cancer, and when he missed a hall duty, Mr. Rookie wrote a letter of reprimand and placed it in his file. He didn't even give Mr. Sleeper a chance to explain why he was on the telephone."

Nellie Newcomer added, "He yelled at Mrs. Slacker and ordered her to meet with me every week. Now she treats me worse than ever. I hate meeting with her, but I have to, or she will get in trouble. I probably will also. It's like having detention. I just sit there with her; she doesn't say anything to me, and I cannot get any work done."

Roger realized it was time for him to quit listening to a conversation that clearly was not intended for his ears. He slowly walked to his office as their meeting continued.

TEACHERS' LOUNGE

"Hey, you hear how many principals it takes to get through the year at Anywhere Middle School?" asked Karl Chameleon, a little softer than usual, as at times lounge conversations can be heard from the hallway.

"C'mon, Chameleon, give it a rest!" someone said.

"TWO, one to start off as Dr. Jekyll, and the next to make Mr. Hyde seem more like Mr. Rogers!"

Groans . . . a chuckle or two.

"That's stupid, Karl, but fairly accurate," someone retorted.

"It's certainly not a wonderful day in this neighborhood for any of us, is it?" said Mildred Morose.

"Certainly not for me," said LaVon Babble. "I'm now struggling to arrange my family's after-school schedule; it's taking a toll on all of us."

"Nellie Newcomer and I are now forced to meet each week," said Judy Slacker. "That girl didn't need my help in the first place. I don't know what to say to her. It's awkward. She's doing just fine, as we all know. And Robo-Rookie's now got her afraid that if she and I miss a meeting, she'll be in his office getting verbally abused as I was."

"We should probably invite her down here every once in a while to get her out of the crosshairs," Karl Chameleon chimed in. "Although you all are a bit hard to digest sometimes, we're not the monsters Rookie makes us out to be."

A few giggles.

"Now I 'represent' that remark," said Mildred. "I wear my recalcitrance with a badge of honor. Just call me 'Queen <u>B</u>,' and we all know that '<u>B</u>' doesn't stand for 'badge'!"

Laughter.

"Hey . . . what are y'all doing over the summer?" Karl Chameleon asked.

"Getting the hell as far away from here as possible!" Edgar Sleeper snorted.

"Amen to that, brother!" said Karl.

"In the old days, I would actually do a bit of summer school. Liked the extra cash, but if you think I'm going to be worried about hallway duty and write-ups for a few thousand extra dollars, I'd rather go out and do something else without having to worry about 'Robo's' wrath and a weekly visit to his whipping post."

The lounge door opened and, with a sheepish look on her face, in walked Nellie Newcomer.

"Hey . . . look who it is," said Mildred Morose. "Sweet Polly Purebred."

"Hi, everyone, I don't mean to disturb you all. Would you mind if I microwaved my Lean Cuisine? Mrs. Savage has moved the front office microwave to the bookroom behind her desk, and I'm not allowed in there. I wouldn't want to disturb Mr. Rookie with something such as this."

"Better than that," said Mildred. "Nuke that thing, then why don't you have a seat with us and enjoy your lunch. We were just talking about you. Don't worry, we won't bite."

Laughter.

"Congrats on your first year, Nellie," said Edgar Sleeper.

"Made it through the gauntlet," said Karl Chameleon.

"She's a good kid," said Judy Slacker.

Although Nellie thought Judy was a bit insincere, she did feel good with the well-wishes. This was a group that intimidated her a bit, but they always seemed to have a good time. Maybe if she spent a bit more time with them, she would earn their respect, and still keep a great professional friendship with Mrs. Starr.

Nellie Newcomer felt camaraderie. It felt good, yet she also felt odd and guilty for visiting the lounge. She was confused.

But she felt welcome.

THE COFFEE KLATCH

Nellie must be tied up today more than usual, thought Sandy Starr. *I can understand that, as the end of a first year is quite trying indeed. I'm so very proud of her.*

Most of the klatch's regulars had gone back to their classrooms, worried about getting their grades submitted in a timely fashion. "Mr. Rookie's got Trudy Savage on 'final grade watch,'" they said. "We're not going to risk incurring the wrath of either."

Sandy Starr then opened her laptop and read an e-mail from the district superintendent announcing the retirements that were to take place, as well as the dates for upcoming congratulatory receptions for those employees.

I must be sure to make a few of these receptions, she thought.

Oh . . . I see from the list that there will be an opening in my content area in another of our middle schools. Gosh . . . over the years, I would have never thought that I wanted to be anywhere else but Anywhere. Yet with the continuing negative nature of many of our staff, coupled with Roger's newfound totalitarianism that is highly disrespectful of all of us, I wonder if I shouldn't use my seniority to make a change. Maybe I'll talk to my husband over dinner tonight.

With that, Sandy Starr began studying the staff roster for the district's other middle school and smiled when she saw a few of the friendly faces she recognized.

PRINCIPAL'S EVALUATION

Roger twiddled his thumbs and doodled nervously while awaiting his year-end evaluation with his superintendent. Thinking back to his charge at the beginning of the year . . .

"What I need you to do immediately in Anywhere Middle School, Rookie, is to change the focus from that of teachers and teaching . . . to that of learning. I want results, not just forming a committee . . . I want that place turned around."

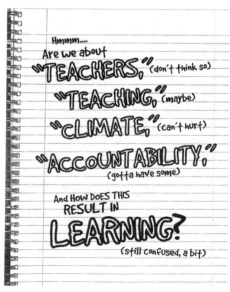

The superintendent's voice echoed in Roger's mind again and again and again as he asked himself, "Am I on track?" Standardized test scores were scheduled to arrive over the summer and, more than anything else, Roger wanted another crack at a reinvention of Anywhere.

There's always that natural "do-over" when fall arrives, he anticipated. *I can't wait to see what we can accomplish, now that I'm settling in to doing some "real leading" with those folks.*

"Roger, can I get you anything to drink while the superintendent finishes with his telephone calls?"

Cindy Sage was always a gracious host for those visiting the Central Office.

Roger had grown to value the time in her office over the past year. Though always nervous in anticipating a visit with his boss, the feel of the outer office was almost like his mom's living room at home. He felt Mrs. Sage was on his side.

"Thank you for that, Mrs. Sage. Yes, I would love some coffee, if it isn't too much trouble."

"Of course not, Roger. Grab that mug right over there; I'll pour if you don't mind."

"Thank you."

"I hear that things have been changing at Anywhere, Roger. You're moving forward with a new leadership style, from what I understand."

Roger, a bit taken aback in that he wondered how she had heard about this, said, "You've heard that, huh?"

"Why, yes Roger. It is the talk of the district."

"I owe a good deal of credit to Mr. Ironside from Blue Collar Middle School," said Roger. "Much as his teachers did for me when I was student teaching in his school, he has personally helped me dig deep into my leadership style, so as to help me move our school forward, as my boss expects."

"How is the new style working for you, Roger? Does it fit you as well as it does Ivan Ironside?"

Roger answered by not answering.

He first told Mrs. Sage about many of the actions that had happened the past ten weeks, doing his best to shine the most positive light on the increased accountability teachers and students felt with respect to their roles in the school.

He shared other positive outcomes, saying, "I have had more productive faculty meetings; staff are doing what I am asking, and The Bullies have quit complaining."

Mrs. Sage then asked, "Have you sought out the advice of any of your superstar teachers on this change of leadership style? That would be very interesting for you in setting some leadership goals for next year, don't you think?"

Roger thought to himself, *Well . . . not really. In fact, in the past three months, I cannot even recall more than two occasions when I have spoken with Sandy Starr. Even my talks with Nellie Newcomer have been more focused on whether she and Judy Slacker had met, as opposed to how everything was going.*

He thought further, *Not one pat on the back . . . not one expression of gratitude . . . and not even one invitation to a faculty social or even a graduating senior's open house. I always thought principals and staffs were supposed do these sorts of things as years ended and summers approached.*

Gosh . . . I have been too busy to even miss that I'm not being included in anything that I'm not demanding others to do.

"Roger . . . Roger . . . are you still with me? You look deep in thought."

"Oh . . . it's nothing, Mrs. Sage; maybe it's just that I'm a bit nervous for my year-end evaluation. I guess we're all nervous when we're being held accountable, aren't we?"

Mrs. Sage shared, "Accountability is critical for any organization to function at a high level, and a school without accountability will never be able to help every student reach his or her potential. A leader without accountability will never grow as a leader. It says much for you to embrace this, Roger."

"I want to ask you a question, however. Do you think that Roger Rookie's leading his school as Ivan Ironside has led his has allowed others to get to know more about you as a leader operating from your core beliefs, or is it causing a dissonance in who you are and who you feel you need to be to accomplish your goals?"

Roger thought deeply.

"To be quite frank, Mrs. Sage, I'm not sure. My staff follows my or-ders, students are more compliant, but I'm not sure that I am leading the way that I thought I would when I first graduated from principal school."

"That may very well be OK," Mrs. Sage responded reassuringly. "We all are finding our way as best we can. We are all bringing the best we know how to school each day, aren't we? That includes our students and staff members, Roger. We are all just people taking our lives one day at a time."

Why Roger flashed instantly to thoughts of LaVon Babble juggling her schedule with her family's needs, he didn't know.

He tried not to think of it, as he had too much on his mind.

"Roger, think of a great leader you know . . . or one you have known at some point in your life."

Roger searched his memory. "That would be Mr. Good, my middle school teacher and coach."

"Why was he great, Roger?"

"Well . . . he had high expectations. He had the ability to develop personal relationships with all of us, while at the same time challenging us to improve performance. When we had individual needs requiring extra consideration, like family problems or hardships, he would work things out as best he could to make reasonable accommodations for us. And . . . he believed in us."

"Roger, great leaders like Mr. Good understand that fundamental to people reaching their potential, they have to be held accountable, which is not always met with appreciation in the heat of the moment. On the other hand, they offer something else to counterbalance this account-ability, something that makes folks want to perform for them in ways that they typically wouldn't do for themselves."

"You know, Mrs. Sage, that makes sense," Roger said with a smile. "Anybody who has been fortunate enough to have a special teacher, coach, mentor, or boss that brought out the best in them had moments during the relationship where they were upset with the constant feed-back on how to improve."

Roger's mind wandered again, as his thoughts were accelerating. *Great leaders demand excellence, and when somebody is not performing to his or her potential, the great leader is going to continue to communi-*

cate why the performance level needs to improve and how they are going to work together for the improvement. But, oh, my goodness, what sets a leader apart from an authoritative manager is that great leaders bring out the best in people, while at the same time engaging in a relationship built on trust and respect.

Mrs. Sage concluded, "In many occasions, Roger, it takes people weeks, months, or even years to appreciate how a great leader was able to get them to perform at levels they did not fully appreciate at the time. Give yourself a pat on the back for doing what you could this past year, as best as you could. After all, didn't you, as did your staff, come to school each day and do the best you knew how?"

Roger felt like he had just experienced a "light bulb" moment.

He was an *either/or* leader trying desperately to address the demands of a *both/and* school.

It was as if Roger Rookie's leadership was swinging like a pendulum, desperately trying to improve a focus on learning, but swinging one way into climate . . . then the other way into accountability. Neither on its own was doing the job in creating a learning-centered environment.

In thinking of the leadership of Mr. Good and others who made a more powerful impact in his life, he knew in a blinding flash of the obvious that he couldn't expect performance to improve with "either/or." He couldn't lead as a pendulum. He certainly couldn't continue putting his thumb on his superstar teachers, who instead needed to be liberated and emulated. Only a "both/and" approach would move things where they needed to go.

Roger announced to Mrs. Sage . . . "I think I'm feeling a lot better about my evaluation today. Thank you."

After his meeting with the superintendent, he hurried home and continued with his deep thoughts.

ROGER ROOKIE'S DEEP THOUGHTS

THE THUMB EFFECTS ON STAFF...

SUPERSTARS
- Feel restricted/stop taking risks
- Cut themselves off from the rest of the school
- Are upset when their colleagues are disrespected

FENCESITTERS
- Align with bullies for protection
- Become overcome with inaction
- Never take a risk

BULLIES
- Move from obvious to subversive
- Provide refuge for others
- Lay in the weeds, waiting to strike!

THE THUMB
CONTINUED...

THE LEADER FEELS
- Empowered at first
- Sad, when he/she realizes the positive people are afraid and avoid him/her
- Completely alone

UNINTENDED CONSEQUENCES
- Good people either side with the bad or want to leave the school
- Everyone works against the leader, or at minimum...wait for mistakes
- Leader loses support of students, parents, staff, and community

That's when it happened! Roger Rookie saw something vividly in his mind's eye that he knew he needed to draw before it left him. The secret was revealing itself in a way that wasn't really even that secretive. Things were now making sense. He drew it on his notebook.

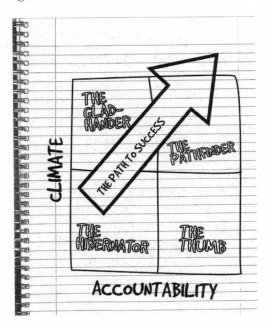

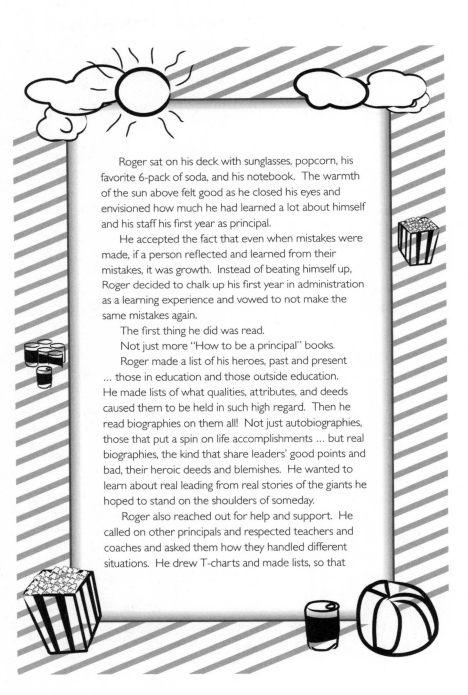

Roger sat on his deck with sunglasses, popcorn, his favorite 6-pack of soda, and his notebook. The warmth of the sun above felt good as he closed his eyes and envisioned how much he had learned a lot about himself and his staff his first year as principal.

He accepted the fact that even when mistakes were made, if a person reflected and learned from their mistakes, it was growth. Instead of beating himself up, Roger decided to chalk up his first year in administration as a learning experience and vowed to not make the same mistakes again.

The first thing he did was read.

Not just more "How to be a principal" books.

Roger made a list of his heroes, past and present ... those in education and those outside education. He made lists of what qualities, attributes, and deeds caused them to be held in such high regard. Then he read biographies on them all! Not just autobiographies, those that put a spin on life accomplishments ... but real biographies, the kind that share leaders' good points and bad, their heroic deeds and blemishes. He wanted to learn about real leading from real stories of the giants he hoped to stand on the shoulders of someday.

Roger also reached out for help and support. He called on other principals and respected teachers and coaches and asked them how they handled different situations. He drew T-charts and made lists, so that he could learn all he could about a healthy balance between accountability and climate.

At times, Roger received completely different responses from leaders. That was ok, as he never reacted or judged the person. He was interested in hearing why leaders chose a particular method or strategy, thinking again as Cindy Sage had mentioned, "We are all bringing the best we know how to school each day, aren't we?"

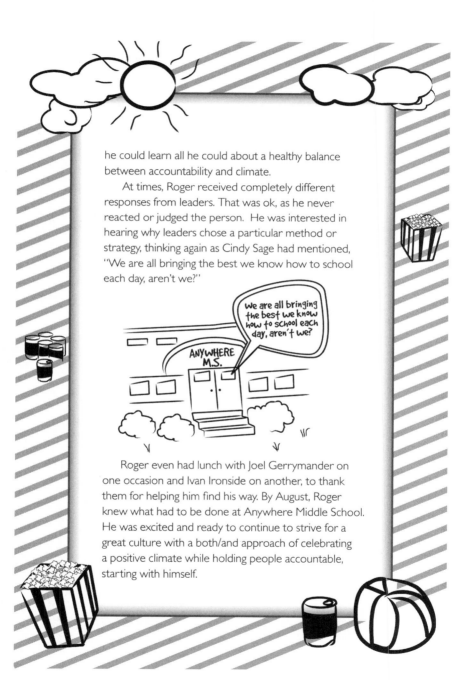

Roger even had lunch with Joel Gerrymander on one occasion and Ivan Ironside on another, to thank them for helping him find his way. By August, Roger knew what had to be done at Anywhere Middle School. He was excited and ready to continue to strive for a great culture with a both/and approach of celebrating a positive climate while holding people accountable, starting with himself.

5

ROGER ROOKIE'S FINAL MAKEOVER: THE PATHFINDER

Roger was ready for his second year as principal. As he walked into his back-to-school faculty meeting, his last thought was, *Together, we will make a difference.* He realized, *I don't have to prove who is in charge; everybody knows who is in charge. And the more I try to prove it, the more everybody tries to prove me wrong.*

"Welcome back, everyone," said Roger Rookie. "Let's all share some of the great things that we all experienced this past summer, after we meet our new staff members."

Staff members were a bit gun-shy.

They didn't share much, as they worried a bit about Roger's reaction to anything they might say. After all, he really did end last year as "The Thumb." Roger could sense the apprehension. He didn't want to pretend that it was invisible to him.

"First, everyone, let me share that I feel a bit of the uneasiness in the room. I understand. You're wondering, first of all, why I'm smiling so much today, and probably . . . legitimately . . . when I'll wipe that smile off my face and begin cracking the whip."

Pocketed murmurs confirmed his perception.

"What I would like you to know about Roger Rookie as we begin this

school year is this. As your principal, I very much appreciate all the guidance and support that you provided to me in my first year"—a comment
true for most of his staff.

"My first year as a principal was much like my first year as a teacher.
It had rewarding moments that validated my decision to be an educator,
yet moments as well when I left school and wondered why I didn't join
the circus."

A few chuckled.

"OR . . . 'the military,' you're probably thinking," Roger added.

Smattering of nervous laughter.

Roger continued, "I love what I do, at least on most days. I always
strive to get better. It took me a few years as a teacher, but eventually
I was told that I did a pretty good job. I pledge to you that I bring that
same attitude to the principal position. We have a great team here at
AMS, and I am really excited for our new school year."

"Please give me the time to show you how I have grown this past summer in reflection of my abilities as a leader, in consideration of the fine job
you all do in leading your classrooms. Welcome, all, to a new beginning!"

Staff members looked around at each other, still uncomfortable . . .
not saying much. Then they turned their attention back to Roger Rookie.

Roger then announced the building leadership team. Over the summer, Roger had contacted a group of teachers that he knew were the
most effective teachers at AMS. He asked each of them to join the
leadership team. As he understood, many of the teachers were leery of
accepting, especially Sandy Starr, but Roger persisted and shared with
the teachers that he would support them and that the school was only
going to go as far as they took it. Eventually, he was able to convince all
of the most effective teachers to be on the leadership team.

"Chairing that team will be Mrs. Sandy Starr," Roger announced with
a smile.

The response to the announcement was immediate. Mildred Morose
asked, "Mr. Rookie, how exactly was the leadership team formed?"

"Mrs. Morose, I contacted teachers personally to serve on the committee, based on the qualities and attributes I felt they had that could
contribute to the mission of the committee's charge."

LaVon Babble inquired quickly, "Other teachers will also serve on the
committee, won't they?"

Roger casually responded, "I appreciate the interest; however, the leadership committee is full this year, but I do know there are other committees that could benefit from your service, Mrs. Babble. Might you be interested in the holiday party planning committee?"

Several staff members were not sure what had just happened.

Roger continued down the agenda.

Edgar Sleeper said, "But, Mr. Rookie . . ."

Roger respectfully said quickly, "No worries, Mr. Sleeper, I'll put you down for the holiday committee as well. Please feel free to see me privately after the meeting if you wish to discuss anything further."

When Roger got to "teacher duties," he paused and reminded himself to be strong.

Roger announced, "Because of the instructional needs of our students, the school will revert back to five more minutes of Seminar time and teachers supervising the commons area before school."

A frenzy of talking began.

Finally, Mildred Morose said in a loud voice, "Why in the world should we get cheated out of five minutes of lunch and have to supervise the commons when we should be preparing for class!?! Last year was the best year I've had in my thirty-year career, and I have no intention of doing a duty that is not asked of high school teachers. If you try to implement these changes, you can expect a grievance!"

As Roger looked around the room, one could hear a pin drop. Very few eyes were able to muster the courage to look at him. Mildred even sat back down.

He said, "Having the paraprofessionals cover lunch and the commons duty last year was a mistake. I take full responsibility. I did it to help teachers because you have such demanding jobs; however, that decision was not in the best interest of our students or the paraprofessionals."

Sandy Starr smiled, giving a nod to Nellie Newcomer.

"We have a great staff that has the training and experience to help our students in all situations. We cannot and will not give the duty to other hard working staff members simply because we do not want to do it."

Sandy Starr raised her hand to speak.

"Yes, Mrs. Starr?"

"I never thought having our paraprofessionals cover our duties was the right thing for our students or our school. Even though I too enjoyed the additional time spent in planning, we need to ensure that we are the ones instructionally and behaviorally supervising our students."

A few nodded.

Sandy Starr continued, "Last year, I noticed an increase in students complaining about name-calling and harassment before school, so I think we'll need to be vigilant from the first day to restore order and be clear about our expectations before school and during lunch."

Roger Rookie could not have said it better.

Later in the meeting, as Roger was discussing the changes in how data would be analyzed, he noticed The Bullies were talking with each other. As he paused, The Bullies continued to talk loudly and draw attention. Roger even heard his name mentioned.

As Roger looked around the room, it was obvious to him that the rest of the staff was not comfortable with what was happening. He kept his composure, as he knew he had to strike a balance between dealing with the issue and treating everybody with respect.

Roger Rookie then walked over to the area of The Bullies, looked Mildred Morose in the eyes and said, "Ladies and gentlemen, may we please have attention at our meeting? We have many important items to discuss, and I value your time in allowing the agenda to continue."

Mildred Morose made a snide remark. Roger did not take the bait. Instead, he thanked them for showing him the same respect that he knew they demanded from their students and repositioned himself in front of the faculty as a whole.

Roger then got to his other big announcement, which he knew would be very unpopular with some staff. He said, "The leadership team and I have discussed the achievement gap between those students with special needs and those without. Beginning this school year, all special education students will receive their reading and math instruction in the regular education classrooms. Staff will utilize a co-teaching model."

The response was what he expected.

One teacher said, "Do you realize the effect the inclusion model will have on the rest of the students?!? What about the effect on the teachers?!? I don't want those kids in my classroom!!"

Another said, "I have concerns trying to co-teach with other teachers in the building."

Roger allowed the staff to share their concerns and kept reiterating that it would be a learning process for all; however, he had worked with the leadership team and the decision had been made.

"We must ensure that each and every decision we make has at its foundation student learning, rather than the way we have always envisioned the structure and delivery of our teaching," Roger emphasized.

He finished discussion by saying, "Please trust in these major decisions that significant professional development time will be made available during the year for the staff to have time to plan and problem solve how best to implement the new service model. Other support agencies will help us implement the co-teaching model that has had such positive results in schools across the country."

Roger was on a roll, so decided to keep announcing changes at AMS.

Roger told the staff that the two new teachers, Nathan Neophyte and Sally Sterling, would both need mentors. "Starting immediately, mentorships will be posted and interested teachers can apply. I will then select mentors that I think will provide the best support for the needs of the teachers."

Teachers took this in stride. Judy Slacker snorted and turned her head.

The rest of the meeting was relatively quiet. Roger walked to his office with a sigh of relief and a little bounce to his step.

UNFINISHED BUSINESS

Later in the day, Roger was dropping off a note in a teacher's mailbox, when he heard Trudy Savage say, "Well, I knew you would finally have to show your chubby-cheeked little face in the office."

Sally Sterling was standing with a nervous look on her face, cheeks admittedly chubby AND a bit flushed with that greeting. Roger had hired Sally over the summer. She reminded him quite a bit of Nellie

Newcomer and he was convinced she was going to be a great teacher for AMS.

Trudy Savage then blared, "Who do you think you are to come into this school and start taking items that do not belong to you?" Sally Sterling lowered her head and did not dare speak.

Roger rushed around the corner, saying, "Mrs. Savage, what is your concern?"

Trudy Savage looked at Roger Rookie dismissively, and then stated as accusatorily as possible, "This girl apparently was raised to think it's OK to take items that do not belong to her. Without asking, she has taken the extra printer we had in the teachers' workroom."

The office was a full house; all looked at Roger Rookie.

Roger said to Sally Sterling, "I am so sorry for this confusion. I told you to take the extra printer for your room; you have done nothing wrong."

Roger then looked at Trudy Savage and said, "Mrs. Savage, will you please accompany me to my office."

There was no mistaking the seriousness in Roger Rookie's tone or the look on his face.

Trudy Savage responded, "You will have to wait as I have several important things I must get done for the children of this community prior to their arrival."

Teachers watched with shock and awe.

Roger then stated, "We will meet in my office in thirty minutes, and you are advised to bring a union representative with you."

Trudy Savage muttered, "I guess the children and everyone else will just have to wait, so that your needs can be met, Mr. Principal!" She left the office to call a union representative.

CLOSED-DOOR MEETING

Roger began the meeting by saying, "Mrs. Savage, what happened with Ms. Sterling will never happen again."

"Won't have to, Mr. Rookie, if you would stop giving printers to all the young women on staff. Must be nice to have friends with benefits?"

Roger maintained his resolve, saying, "Aside from your continued unprofessionalism, Mrs. Savage, your interpersonal skills with students, staff and community members have been unsatisfactory and must improve immediately. I will begin drafting an improvement plan that will be very specific in the areas of concern and the specific actions you must take to be successful."

With that, Trudy Savage pointed her finger at Roger and told him that she loved the students who deserved, and further, had earned the respect of the staff. "The ONLY parents that do not appreciate the way I conduct myself are the no-good, irresponsible parents that do not deserve to be treated with kindness. And . . . I might add, they should have practiced better birth control."

What on earth has created this angry, foul, person?!? Roger thought to himself. *It's just unbelievable!*

Trudy Savage finished her verbal onslaught by jabbing a finger in Roger's chest, stating, "I have been at Anywhere Middle School long before your arrival and will be here long after you are gone."

Roger counted to ten before he spoke, wanting to let the intensity of Trudy's actions diminish. He couldn't believe what just happened. He got thumped in the chest by one of his employees.

Then he calmly said, "Mrs. Savage, you are being suspended from work for, in part, conduct unbecoming an educator, and you will be put on paid administrative leave pending an investigation and deliberation for potential further discipline. Further, you are to submit to me your keys and leave immediately. Any further misconduct will lead to additional discipline."

For the first time in her career, Trudy Savage had no response.

Roger emphasized, "You are not permitted on school property until further notice. Someone from Central Office will be contacting you within three days, and you will be given due process during the handling of these incidents. I will walk you to the exit."

Trudy Savage began to speak, but thought better of it.

She threw her keys on Roger's desk and defiantly stormed out of her office.

Roger stayed a few feet behind, but escorted her off the property.

Several teachers were in the office and tried to look busy while watching them walk to the edge of the property. "It's about time Trudy

Savage walked her own 'Green Mile,'" someone said. Word spread like wildfire.

After Trudy Savage was gone, Roger Rookie returned to the building and went immediately to Sally Sterling's room to apologize again for Trudy's behavior and make sure she was OK.

At the end of the day, Roger returned to his office and noticed his voice message light on his phone was blinking. The message was from the associate superintendent.

It said, "Roger, I would like to inform you that a Mrs. Mildred Morose from your school had contacted me to complain about your taking time from their lunch and implementing a special education system without any staff input or support. I want to assure you, Roger, that after reviewing our policies and agreements we have in place, I am not concerned with the complaint. I just wanted you to be aware that a call came from your building. Please know that I have complete confidence in you. It's about time somebody started leading the AMS staff. Have a great start to the school year."

Roger smiled and played the message a second time.

OUT AND ABOUT

The next day, Roger was in Nellie Newcomer's room first thing in the morning with her favorite drink, a large chai tea.

Nellie smiled, "Thank you, Mr. Rookie, for the tea."

Roger began, "I am here today to apologize to you. Last year was your first year, and I did a poor job of providing you with support you needed and deserved. However, I am determined to make it right. Although it is your second year and you are on my leadership team, which indicates my level of respect for you, I have asked Mrs. Starr to serve as your mentor this year. You are a really good teacher, Nellie, and with a little bit of coaching, you will be a great teacher. I predict you will be serving as a mentor in a few years."

Nellie Newcomer responded, "Thank you so much, Mr. Rookie. I want you to know as well that I went home really excited yesterday, as I could tell from how you led the faculty meeting that this is going to be a special year at AMS."

Roger smiled. "Nellie, I'll be checking in frequently to see what else there is that I can provide for you. Thanks for all you do."

Roger then walked around the school and observed teachers working frantically on last-minute details for the first day of school. As Roger walked into Karl Chameleon's room, he said, "Karl, tell me more about your trip that you mentioned briefly at staff meeting."

"Went to Yellowstone, saw the sights . . . did all the fun stuff. Took in a geyser!! Definitely a special end of the world out there," Karl responded, talking at length for a good ten minutes. When Karl finished, Roger asked, "What's all this, Karl? Your classroom really looks different!"

Roger Rookie noticed that Karl Chameleon had actually decorated his classroom. Last year Karl's room was pretty bland; this year it had a major makeover.

Karl responded, "After our last summer leadership meeting, I asked Mrs. Starr about her room, and she gave me several great ideas on surrounding students with motivation, including student work. I have to say, I think my room looks a lot better."

"Sure does, Karl. It looks GREAT."

"I was also very excited last summer, Karl, when you accepted the offer to be on our leadership team. Folks really like you, Karl, and your ideas are top-notch! We just need to give you more opportunities to share them with people who will add value to the conversation and help to make them a reality. I think our team will do 'just that.'"

BUILDING LEADERSHIP TEAM MEETING

The building leadership team met for its monthly meeting, reviewing several of the changes Roger Rookie communicated at the faculty meeting at the beginning of the year. When the agenda shifted to New Items, Sandy Starr brought up the reading series that had unanimous support from the leadership team, the same series that Roger squashed last year.

Roger looked around the room and said, "First, we have to review the curriculum. Which team members would be willing to meet and go over the curriculum with me?"

Sandy enthusiastically raised her hand along with a couple of other members of the leadership team.

"Fantastic!"

Roger continued, "It will challenge our budget, but if this group thinks the new curriculum is a good idea, then I will do everything possible to make it happen. Yours is a focus on learning that I must value more as your leader."

Roger then asked, "Do you still feel that the professional development that we had been discussing over the summer months—that focused on the new special education delivery plan—is where we should concentrate our efforts and expenditures?"

"Absolutely, Mr. Rookie," said Nellie Newcomer.

"Sure thing," Karl Chameleon added.

"Would agree," said Sandy Starr.

They all concurred that a focus on providing significant support and resources for staff in a new model of instruction was critical. The remainder of the meeting was spent planning for supporting staff with the change. Meeting with this group of mission-mindful professionals reenergized Roger and helped him focus on the important things.

NEW BUSINESS AS USUAL

Roger could not believe that two months of school had already passed. He felt that one of the biggest mistakes he made in his first year as principal was the decision to "get tough" with students, as it had a negative impact it had on his relationship with students and parents. Frankly, it stymied communication.

Roger now ensured that, while working with students in disciplinary situations, he would focus not only on accountability for one's actions as a stepping stone to learning about responsibility, but also on the climate of the conversation as a learning experience. Giving students an opportunity to speak and asking them a series of questions so they could reflect on their actions and/or behaviors almost always led to students' figuring out what they would need to do in the future to avoid making poor choices. This made for much better school, family, and community partnerships.

Another "light bulb moment" in balancing climate and accountability was when one or two staff members were doing something unsatisfactory, like showing up late for work, for example, Roger now NEVER communicated the problem as if everybody was doing something wrong. Roger's former methods of sending mass school-wide e-mails or making announcements about a problem made his most effective teachers feel uncomfortable, because they immediately remembered the one time they showed up late. Conversely, the employees who show up late frequently disregarded the mass communication and actually found protective cover in it. They would think, *Hah! I must not be the only one.*

In just a short period of time, Roger already had a handful of "opportunities" to put his new individualized problem-solving feedback into practice.

BALANCING CLIMATE WITH ACCOUNTABILITY

During a late-fall workshop, Roger met with all teachers who were to be evaluated. Many of the teachers knew it was "their year," and Roger Rookie had wanted to give them a bit of space early on to get things off the ground. However, two teachers were surprised to learn that they were being evaluated. Roger agreed to meet with each individually to explain why this had occurred, responding that "every three years" was the "minimum" for evaluation.

Roger said to each, "Because I believe that, as your instructional leader, I can provide the support and supervision to help you improve in key areas, a formal evaluation process is the appropriate method to address the areas of concern. It keeps us all on the same page, and that page focuses on student learning."

Roger was getting ready to have his post-observation conference with one of the teachers he had added to the list, Mildred Morose.

Roger began, "Mrs. Morose, what are your thoughts on the lesson?"

Mildred replied, "Well, of course it was a good lesson, given the students I have worked with this year, Roger."

Roger probed deeper, "What exactly do you mean, Mrs. Morose?"

Her trademark frown appeared, "Isn't it obvious that we have a disadvantage at AMS? Our students don't come to school prepared, and I can tell you why, as I had most of their parents in school, and they were no picnic either. Guess what, the apples did not fall far from the trees. It's basic biology, really."

Roger shook his head in disbelief.

"Mrs. Morose, you have the same students as all the other teachers here at AMS, yet your student achievement data is consistently lower than your peers. You contend that students are the variable, but I believe that you as the teacher own some of this responsibility as well."

He continued, "A good teacher finds a way to help all students learn. Mrs. Morose, I am going to draft an improvement plan with you and provide you with the necessary support and resources to improve your teaching. If you are willing to change your instructional practices, I know you can be a quality teacher; however, it is going to require you to do things differently."

Mildred's blood began to boil.

"Rookie, if I knew this meeting was going to include you threatening to fire me, I would have brought my union representative. What you are doing is illegal, and I can probably get you fired."

Roger did not respond. He simply got up, walked toward the door, turned to Mildred Morose, and said, "I'll begin drafting the improvement plan. Oh, and yes . . . as a courtesy to you, I will remember to include your union representative when I schedule our next meeting."

Roger Rookie left the room.

Roger Rookie was walking around AMS when Karl Chameleon waved him in. Roger was pleased with the significant changes in Karl's teaching and overall attitude and was, in fact, amazed how much a teacher could transform himself in one year with the right attitude and support.

After small talk about the upcoming Thanksgiving break, Karl told Roger, "There is something I want to visit with you about, boss, but I'm a little hesitant."

Roger asked, "What's holding you back?"

"Well, you have been great to work with this year, but I am still reminded of how radically different your leadership styles were last year, and after all, you are my boss."

Roger laughed and responded, "Fair enough, point taken, Karl. Please, share with me what's on your mind. I promise not to go 'Mr. Hyde' on you."

Karl did a quick double take, thinking of the teachers' lounge, but kept on point.

"Remember that conversation last year about calculators?"

"Yes, I recall the conversation vividly. I probably told you I would consider it, or we didn't have enough money."

The look on Karl's face told Roger his memory was accurate.

"Hey . . . do you still need them?"

"Mr. Rookie, our students really do. In fact, some of the math that students are supposed to know for their high-stakes tests requires that they know how to use those special functions that only the graphing calculators provide. Our current calculators are simply unequipped. They're not helping the learning."

"No kidding."

"Yep, Mr. Rookie. . . . What used to be a 'want' is now truly a 'need.'"

Roger assured Karl, "I'll find a way to get you a classroom set of calculators, and if I am unsuccessful, it will be my fault. Learning centeredness starts with the principal."

Karl Chameleon thanked Roger Rookie for listening and supporting him. After a high-five, Roger continued visiting teachers in their classrooms, striving for a balance of climate and accountability as he moved through the year as an instructional leader.

CONCLUDING YEAR TWO

When the superintendent walked in Roger's front office at Anywhere Middle School, new secretary Kris Bliss greeted him. It had been seven months since the board of education had acted on Trudy Savage's resignation, and since then Kris had moved to the main secretary chair and the district had hired Joy Daily as the other secretary.

Trudy Savage's resignation piqued the interest of the superintendent to see firsthand what Roger Rookie was doing. Something was actually "done" about a problem, and he liked that.

I'll take a Rookie over a Neverthere any day, he mused.

Roger Rookie walked in while the superintendent was reading several thank-you letters that Roger had received from students and parents and that were displayed on the wall in his office.

The superintendent quickly turned and asked, "Rookie, how are things going over here? Be straight with me. Give me the facts. Do we have a focus on learning or is it just smoke and mirrors, and a little bit of Rookie luck on your part!?!"

Roger paused, and then said, "Things are going really well. I'm not going to lie; we have a lot more work to do, but the leadership team has established some ambitious goals, and I could not be more proud of the staff for the effort they give everyday to help our students. Our conversations revolve around learning."

"What about leadership, Rookie!? So yeah . . . you can move out a secretary with an anger management problem, but can you lead PEOPLE? Can you get the Joe Averages and Martha Middle-of-the-Roads to perform and raise those test scores?!?"

"Well, number one, sir . . . I think I have found the secret AND the path to a school focus on learning. I have found that, with every notch that I ratchet up accountability, I need to do the same with climate. They work in tandem, and by doing both, enhanced learning becomes the focus of conversation. This takes time, but we're moving ahead."

"Here, let me show you." Roger pulled out his notebook and turned to the following page:

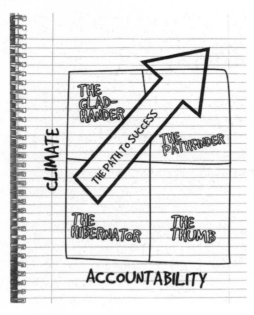

"Don't give me a grad school lecture, Rookie, just tell me how you're doing it! You say you've got the secret? Give me an example of how it works in plain English!"

"First of all, sir, Kris Bliss taking over in the front office has been one of the biggest reasons the climate of the school is changing so quickly and dramatically. Joy Daily is a big help as well. Because of the hundreds of telephone conversations and front-desk visits they have each week, parents really feel that our school is on their side. They then support us when we ratchet up accountability, whether it's in our requesting that they come to parent-teacher conferences or checking on homework in book bags each night."

Roger continued, "When faculty or staff come to the office, Kris and Joy do what they can to immediately make their professional lives better, and this frees up staff to concentrate on what they do best—educating kids and holding themselves accountable for the learning that takes place."

"Yeah . . . yeah . . . yeah . . . I can see where everybody holding hands and singing, 'We are the World' has its benefits, so tell me what else is working. Get to the meat and potatoes, Rookie!"

"OK, sir . . . The Bullies are no longer running the school."

"Wait, Rookie . . . I haven't heard that term in years. I think I started teaching with some of them! Are Morose and Slacker still around, sucking air and squandering my tax dollars?!? Didn't I fix that with an early retirement incentive a few years back?"

Roger reassured him, "They're still here, sir; however, I placed Mildred Morose on an improvement plan and am hopeful that with support, she will make the necessary improvements and begin thinking about students' needs and not her own personal needs. Judy Slacker has yet to get on board, but she is no longer outwardly causing trouble. Oh . . . you may or may not know them, but two of their Bullies-in-Training, Edgar Sleeper and LaVon Babble, have already left the group, and, although they still require a lot of attention and support, they are joining the AMS team and have embraced the changes we have implemented."

"Just don't be afraid to send me another name for a board meeting, Rookie, if you need to hike up your breeches and get rid of someone else!"

"I'll not hesitate, sir."

"Rookie . . . let me tell you something. After seeing what's been going on around here, I'm here to tell you that the biggest reason this school is headed in the right direction is because the students and staff are finally getting the leadership they deserve and no, I'm not talking about you! Well, OK . . . you're part of it. But ALL STAFF are now ensuring leadership at ALL levels. It's trickling down to students. By your work in getting the jerks and losers out of the way . . . our most effective teachers are taking active roles as leaders."

"Thank you, sir, for noticing."

"That's the beginning of a new day at Anywhere, Rookie. A focus on learning that I hope continues long after I'm greeting folks at the shopping center down the street."

As the superintendent left for other buildings, Roger thought to himself about the shifting paradigm that a focus on both climate and accountability had created. And . . . how a focus on learning is moving in the right direction.

He reflected to himself, *Don't get me wrong; we still have passionate discussions at meetings, except now we are no longer wasting time debating who should cover lunch duty. Instead we spend our limited professional development time in collaborative teams reviewing data, discussing instruction, and helping our students ensure better learning.*

When a student or staff member does something worthy of celebration, we celebrate. We have dedicated and caring teachers serving as mentors, teaching and modeling to our beginning teachers that we are in education to help students. We are collectively focused on learning at Anywhere Middle School.

Mindful of such, Roger's leadership team hosted Anywhere Middle School's first all-school academic assembly near the end of his second school year to congratulate students and staff for the improvements made on the curriculum-based assessments as well as for their classroom grades. They anticipated higher standardized achievement test results to arrive over the summer. They also commended faculty on the co-teaching model, as they had no idea it would benefit all AMS students so quickly and dramatically.

Data on achievement were now climbing . . . at this rate, in another few years, scores would be through the roof. Great things were taking on a life of their own, as the leadership team and entire faculty were now starting to have better conversations about teaching and learning.

Don't get me wrong, Roger thought. *Anywhere Middle School has a lot of room for improvement, and if we fall short of the lofty goals we set, it won't be for a lack of effort. However, with attention to both climate and accountability, our learning centeredness has created a refreshing shift from focusing on the needs of adults to focusing on the needs of students. As long as we continue doing that, good things will happen.*

TEACHERS' LOUNGE

"What in the heck are you doing with that 'connect-the-dots' contraption, Mildred?" asked Judy Slacker. "You're beginning to worry me!"

"It's a pacing guide for my curriculum, Slacker. You should know that. Better take a good long look . . . one of these darned things is going to be in your future as well. You're on Rookie's rotation for next fall's evaluations, and he'll put you on the clock."

"Sure . . . just let him try. I operate on one time clock—Slacker Standard Time."

"Yeah . . . yeah . . . yeah, . . ." said Mildred Morose.

"Hey . . . where's everybody today?"

THE COFFEE KLATCH

"Hey . . . you guys hear the one about how many principals it takes to win the pie eating contest at the school pep assembly?" asked Karl Chameleon.

"Better be careful, Karl," smiled Nellie. "With all those calculators that Mr. Rookie just bought for you, you'd be ill-advised in his hearing your wisecracks about beating him in the pep assembly's tricycle race or the kids' shaving his head after those gains in our reading levels."

"Yeah . . . he was a pretty good sport, wasn't he?" said Karl.

"I'm actually going to miss the boss a bit this summer. We're heading to the Florida Keys this year. Can't wait!!"

"Just make sure you schedule your family trip around our leadership team retreat if you can," said Sandy Starr. "Mr. Rookie is pulling out all the stops with some team building. Rumor has it that whitewater rafting is involved."

"That will be great!" said Nellie Newcomer.

"Hey, everybody!!" said Edgar Sleeper on entering.

"Edgarrrrrrrrr," all said in unison.

Edgar loved coming to a place where everybody knew his name. His favorite coffee made his way was quickly set in front of him. He took a sip.

"I can't stay long, guys," said Edgar. "Got my evaluation appointment with Mr. Rookie today, and I think he'll be quite happy with my work on assessments. Just wanted to say 'Hey.' Have a great summer if I don't see you all before."

Edgar downed the coffee quickly and left.

"I'm really glad he came," said Nellie.

"Great guy," said Karl. "You hear the way kids are talking about his class lately?"

Sandy Starr smiled. *It feels good to be around such positive people*, she thought to herself. Nellie Newcomer had been a big part of Sandy Starr's own transformation this past year, as she found she was getting as much out of the mentor/protégé relationship as was Nellie.

The chemistry was just right! It was a catalyst to building-wide camaraderie.

Sandy thought to herself as she poured her last cup of coffee for the year, *Nellie sure is growing in her own leadership. We're becoming so much more like her than how we used to be. That's so important in what we do.*

BACK TO THE BIG NIGHT . . . "THAT'S A WRAP"

"That's simply an incredible story, Roger," said Carol Charming.

"I can really see why you're being given the Super Apple Award by your state principals' association. You not only changed and grew yourself as a leader, but it also appears that by your figuring out the secret in moving down the path to a learning-centered school, everyone at Anywhere Middle School is changing for the good of your entire community."

"Well, thank you, Carol. But again . . . I'm just so very lucky that my staff gave me a chance, that I had room to make my own mistakes, and when I failed, I 'failed forward,' discovering for myself the secret to better learning and leadership, with some wonderful advice and guidance along the way."

"Plus, I get to meet great folks like yourself, Carol! That's certainly a bonus."

"Mr. Rookie . . . two minutes before your introduction on stage," said Kris Bliss, who was at his side and coordinating everything she could—seamlessly, pleasantly, and responsibly.

"Carol . . . you'll love hearing Mr. Rookie when he speaks," said Kris. "He is very inspirational."

"Ms. Bliss needs to do more under-promising, so that I can have a chance of over-delivering," Roger said, with a chuckle, to Carol.

"You are so funny, Roger. I'd better let you go and get back to my place in the reporters' pool, but aside from this story, can I ask you a question?"

"Sure, Carol."

"Would you mind if we got together next week for a quick snack or soda, just to hang out? I work a lot of hours like you, so my schedule is pretty tight, but they have a new place in town called The Popcorn Wagon just down the street. One hundred different flavors—my favorite is Kettle Corn #3. It's just that I'm so glad to meet you and would like to get to know you better, if you don't mind."

Wow . . . Roger thought. The Popcorn Wagon! I've been so busy lately, I haven't had much time to think about stuff like hanging out, let alone with a really cute, young reporter who thinks I'm an "OK" guy.

"I'd love to, Carol! It would be awesome."

Carol Charming then strolled gingerly to the press area with her notepad, offering Roger a warm smile and a wave as he walked to the podium.

ROGER ROOKIE'S DEEP THOUGHTS

THE PATHFINDER'S EFFECTS ON STAFF...

SUPERSTARS
- Feel empowered
- Have unlimited energy
- Willingly take chances and collaborate

FENCESITTERS
- Move toward the superstars
- Want to associate with a winner
- Try harder than they thought possible...collaborate...and LIKE IT!

BULLIES
- Have dramatically reduced power and influence
- Change or leave
- Become very isolated

THE PATHFINDER'S CONTINUED...

THE LEADER FEELS
- Great Satisfaction
- Ready to take on the NEXT CHALLENGE
- PROUD!

UNINTENDED CONSEQUENCES
- Everybody wants to work at your school
- Instead of the leader being the only source of morale, it now comes from everywhere
- FAME, FORTUNE, AND YOU GET THE GIRL!!! ☺